Toward a Spirituality for Global Justice: A Call to Kinship

Toward a Spirituality for Global Justice: A Call to Kinship

Elaine Prevallet

Louisville, Kentucky

Interior design by Kirby Gann
Cover design by P. Dean Pearson

Cover images: Birds/istockphoto; Crowd/istockphoto; Fish/istockphoto; Flowers/P. Dean Pearson.

ISBN 0-9765203-0-3

First Edition
Published by Sowers Books and Videos, a division of Just Faith, Inc. Louisville, Kentucky

Contents

Part I

A New Sense of Unity:
The Call to Global Justice

Chapter One

Reconsidering Our Identity as Humans

*What are human beings that you are mindful of them,
mortals that you care for them?*

Ps. 8:4

*It takes more than a moment to fully realize that this
is Earth . . . home.*

Astronaut Edgar Mitchell

A stronauts from the many nations who ventured into outer space in the last decades spoke of being stunned by the beauty of Earth. To James Irwin, Earth looked like a Christmas tree ornament. "That beautiful, warm, living object," he wrote, "looked so fragile, so delicate, that if you touched it with a finger it would crumble and fall apart." To Edgar Mitchell, it was "a sparkling blue and white jewel, . . . a small pearl in a thick sea of black mystery. It takes more than a moment," he said, "to fully realize this is Earth . . . home." The astronauts felt their perception expand, shifting from seeing at first only their own countries, then continents, and "by the fifth day we were aware of only one Earth." A Syrian astronaut, Muhammad Ahmad Faris, spoke of the planet as "indescribably beautiful with the scars of national boundaries gone." These men sensed the Earth as small, fragile, vulnerable. They experienced a kind of tenderness and care for the whole planet; they felt a new appreciation for its uniqueness, and a sense of responsibility for its well-being.[1]

3

Probably all of us have now seen photos or movies of Earth from outer space. Perhaps, at some level of our awareness, we have felt that same awe, the same tenderness and loyalty as that expressed by the astronauts. We begin to understand and maybe even to feel that Earth is our home.

Here we are. Planet Earth is, after all, only one relatively small planet shining amid hundreds of billions of stars, a tiny part of one single galaxy among billions of galaxies—about many of which we know nothing. And yet, here we sit, thinking, loving, laughing, learning, hurting, celebrating, being born, and dying atop a planet spinning at a pace so fast we cannot feel it, floating around in a space so immense we cannot begin even to imagine it. Instead of spinning off into space as a speck of dust, we are held close to Earth, and to each other, by a mysterious force we name gravity.

What are the chances that *you* should be here, given that you started from one egg cell, chosen from among four hundred thousand others in your mother's womb, by one particular sperm cell from among hundreds of millions produced each day by your father? Doesn't it take your breath away to realize how very improbable, and how precious, is every single fragment of creation?

Who are we, anyway, human members of one of the youngest species, which has been around for only some two hundred thousand years? Have we lost touch with the fact that all other species had, for ages before our arrival, been creating an environment in which we humans could breathe, eat, quench our thirst, survive and even thrive, and that without them we cannot breathe, or eat, or survive, let alone thrive? What is our relationship to all these others—human as well as nonhuman—upon whom we depend for life itself?

We humans, along with all the other species, make up one

earth family, one community of life: that is a fact. So maybe, instead of viewing the rest of the planet as our "resources" to be used in whatever way we choose, we humans need to name all creatures as "our relations," the way some Native peoples do. If all the other species are our relatives—our brothers and sisters (as Francis of Assisi addressed them)—we should want to get to know them, respect and appreciate our essential connection with them, and want them to be able to make their own unique contribution to the good of the whole.

Such a renaming of the relationship would, indeed, signal a major shift in our perception. We would have to rethink our notions of justice in a way that would help us discover how to live in "right relation" to a much more encompassing whole. More than that, we would have to open our hearts to a new universe. We would have to broaden the scope of our moral passions to include the whole world. How would we then experience our responsibility as humans on Earth to all our fellow creatures, all of us held in being, at every moment, by our awesome, continually creating God?

Apparently, we are being drawn forward to enlarge our frame, to change the lenses of our glasses, as it were. Are we beginning to see, really *see*, that our future as a planet hinges on the kinds of decisions we make now, on our willingness to develop ways of cooperating with each other? Are we on the threshold of a new vision, a vision of us all as one world, one planet, all of us connected? Can we begin to look, as the astronauts looked, beyond national boundaries, to enlarge our sense of loyalty, and to ask what it means to be a "global" citizen, to think together and work together for a global common good? Are we beginning to recognize that the violence of war is useless in the long run? What does it mean to "do justice" with the whole planet in view? What kinds of organizations or networks will be helpful? How can we come to some common understanding about how to conduct our human lives in relation to *all* species on planet Earth? And will we have the courage to let that understanding engage our hearts and change our lives?

There is some evidence that the human species is being nudged to move in that direction, broadening our human minds and hearts to embrace as brothers and sisters all humans on the planet, and even all other species. The development of a universally accepted UN Declaration of Human Rights in 1948 was a profound breakthrough in our human history. The very concepts of the United Nations, of an International Court of Criminal Justice, of "international peace-keeping forces"—each of these developments witnesses to a recognition of the need for cooperative relationships and humane patterns of behavior, not just between individuals but among nations. Recently, the populist-generated Earth Charter expresses human hope for a world in which the rights of all species would be recognized and protected. Youngest of all are the beginning steps toward developing a system of law that would be universally recognized and that would take as its basic premise not individual rights and ownership, but genuine *global* justice, governing principles for a world committed to respectful, cooperative relationships honoring not just all nations, but all species.[2] There are signs that we are groping our way toward a sense of global citizenship.

At some level, we already experience what it means to be "one world." We wear clothes that have labels from all over the world; we eat at "ethnic restaurants" featuring food from various countries. We see on TV pictures of people and situations from everywhere, and hear about what is happening. By the Internet we connect in a minute's time with people at a great distance; we carry cell phones and talk to our spouses at home while we're at the airport. Being global citizens has already changed our lifestyle. But has its meaning touched our hearts? What would it mean to be a global citizen from the inside out?

We do have some models. Humanitarian organizations such as Human Rights Watch, Amnesty International, Doctors without Borders, International Red Cross; social and economic organizations of the UN like UNRA, UNHCR, and UNICEF, as well as environmental organizations like Greenpeace: all of these offer evidence of a willingness of some members of the human species to set aside nationality, ethnicity, race, and religious and political opinions—and even species loyalty—and to put themselves at the service of at-risk populations. Faith-based groups devoted to peacemaking and to supplying food, shelter, medicine, and education; groups that attempt to chart in theory and practice the path of religious plurality: all of these groups are pockets of hope that help us imagine some of the qualities that must characterize genuine global citizenship.

The Christian churches have also begun collective efforts to recognize and address the fact that the world now presents a completely new and unprecedented context in which to interpret and express our faith.[3] For the Catholic Church of the modern era, probably the first official indication of the need to rethink the relationship of the church to the world appeared in the late nineteenth century. Pope Leo XIII, in an encyclical entitled *Rerum Novarum*, addressed questions of inequality in relations between owners and workers, encouraging workers to organize for fair wages and decent working conditions. Forty years later, in 1931, in the midst of the Great Depression, Pius XI addressed the universal church in the encyclical *Quadragesimo Anno*, in which he spoke of the necessity for social justice in areas of property ownership and the need for more just distribution of wealth and capital. He promoted the principle of subsidiarity, that is, the right of every person to participate in processes that affect his or her life. These documents marked the beginning of a formal body of "Catholic social teaching," systematic moral reflection by the church's hierarchy on the increasingly complex economic and social problems that confront the church in the modern world.

But the most profound change in the Catholic Church came with the Second Vatican Council, beginning in 1965. The beginning words of the document *Gaudium et Spes* laid out the challenge: "The joys and hopes, the griefs and anxieties of the people of this age, especially those who are poor or in any way afflicted, these too are the joys and hopes, the griefs and anxieties of the followers of Christ." These words were an invitation to broaden the frame of our Christian concerns, to open our hearts to the expanding world, with all of its complex problems and opportunities. Following Pope John XXIII, recent popes, as well as synods of bishops of many nations, have addressed themselves to applying faith to a wide variety of social, political, and economic situations. Two statements were especially noteworthy. The first was the phrase "preferential option for the poor," used by the Latin American bishops at Medellín in 1968, and later adapted to "preferential *love* for the poor." The second, from the synodal document "Justice in the World," issued by the bishops gathered in Rome in 1971, declared that "action on behalf of justice and participation in the transformation of the world" is *"a constitutive dimension of the preaching of the gospel"* (20, italics added), and insisted that "Christian love of neighbor and justice cannot be separated" (34). This statement virtually eliminated the dualism that heretofore separated the church from the world, and challenged Catholics to understand themselves as the church *in* the world. Pastoral letters on peace and economics, issued by the U.S. bishops in 1983 and 1986, continued to provide leadership in the ongoing re-visioning of the church's responsibility vis-à-vis the world. These statements have had a profound impact on the social conscience of many Catholic people.

Catholics have learned to expect and appreciate the reflections on war and peace, economic development, human rights and workers' rights, poverty, structures of injustice, and, recently, ecological concerns. Gender issues and issues of sexual orientation have also been addressed. Although the documents are not infrequently sources of contention and disagreement, Catholics have learned to use them as catalysts for the development of a social conscience, and this body of teaching constitutes a rich heritage in the Catholic tradition.

What is important here is the church's willingness to take seriously the emerging new global awareness that confronts us. Even now, forty years after Vatican II, we are still struggling to integrate the council's recognition that the church is *in* the world, and that we, as church, bear our portion of responsibility for the course of Earth's history and the fate of the community of life on planet Earth. But this struggle appears to be part of a much larger picture.

In fact, we may say that all of the developments, movements, organizations, and official pronouncements we have mentioned above are responses to a nudging of the Holy Spirit, seeking to draw the world into unity. They give evidence of growing awareness of global concerns that cuts across social, national, and religious boundaries, and they challenge us to enlarge the boundaries of our minds and hearts. They prod us to recognize in every single human being, and indeed in every particle of creation, the flesh-and-blood relationship of sister or brother, and to begin the massive task of envisioning what it means to "do justice" in a planetary context. If we must learn to think of the whole community of life as "our relations," what do "right relations" look like in this expanded frame?

Let's imagine a different world. Humans, let's imagine, have finally recognized that while they do have some new and unusual gifts, they are in fact an immensely vulnerable species: they are completely dependent upon all the rest of creation for their life support system! They have recognized that their very strength and their advantage is grounded in connections with the whole earth community—that if they are to flourish as humans, they have to nourish those connections rather than destroy them! And let's imagine, then, that humans have understood that because their species has these new gifts of being able to be conscious and aware—and even more, to experience love and compassion—that they are intended, in the broad, forward-moving sweep of creation, to transform the whole of creation in a harmonious unity by means of compassionate, encompassing awareness and love. And what if humans began to work on their own more primitive instincts of fear, of hoarding, of territoriality, of competition and aggression, of hostility and violence; what if they worked together to develop capacities of sharing, collaboration, mediation, negotiation, peace-making, and harmonization of goals? What if we humans cultivated the skill of turning "threats" into challenges; what if we were prepared to help each other move through our responses of fear and resistance, and learned to elicit life instead of death from situations of tension and threat? What would "right relations" and "justice" involve if we thought of our role on the planet in this way? What if we understood that our planet is held in existence by a single, continuously creative and life-giving Source?

Such a broadened perspective can be a little scary—or awesome. It would shake and undermine our usual ways of defining, thinking, and operating in the world. But such a change is not simply a matter of reason, concepts, or information. Such a change would have to reach us at the deep level of our moral passions. It would involve a complete revolution in our sensibilities, our affective way of relating to the world. We would have to confront ourselves. Why do we not care enough about a future for our children, and indeed for our planetary community of life? Why do we not experience effective moral outrage at pollution and deforestation and species extinction, as well as at nuclear weapons, militarization, and genocides, to name a few? How can we be indifferent, apathetic, nonresponsive in the face of such insults to life itself? What has blinded us? What has de-sensitized us? What has paralyzed us? We would be opening ourselves to a moral revolution, to *metanoia*—a complete change of mind and heart.

But such a change could bring with it a deep sense of renewal, and impart fresh, new energy to every dimension of our lives. In any case, the fact is that our willingness to engage in such a radical change is now a matter of survival.

Justice, or right relations, will have to be considered from a new and very broad, inclusive standpoint. It seems that in this new vision, we may be seeing evidence of the presence and work of the Holy Spirit, whose role is to draw the whole creation into a new and sacred unity. Our rational, scientific processes in the West have, for the first time, presented us with a vision of the world very similar to the vision that lies at the heart of our religious traditions. Scientific explorations of outer space, as well as the hints that physicists glean of the inner space of matter, are proving to be in near-perfect correspondence with the deep inner space of human consciousness and love, residing in the religious traditions of the world and known to us as mysticism.

Western cultures have generally emphasized our need, as human beings, to become strong, independent individuals. Little by little, urged on by the advertising industry, we have begun to act as if our lives depend upon consuming: getting more, having more, eating more. More, more, more.

But now we are realizing that we live on one small, round, limited planet. Mother Earth is showing signs of abuse and exhaustion. We humans have to come to our senses and now see that our lives are out of sync with the rest of creation.

So it is fortunate—or providential—that at this moment of crisis, Western science has opened to our senses, our reasons, and our imaginations a view of the world that is essentially weblike, an interconnected and unified whole. Having been mired in the assumption that our independence as separate individuals was the primary value, we are now being challenged by science itself to reimagine and redefine our human species as one among others, inseparable from the rest of reality. Quantum physics shows us a universe that is continually interactive, involved at every moment in change and exchange, relations that are always characterized by an essential reciprocity and mutuality, a universe that is always in process of breaking down and re-creating. Molecules exchange energy with each other; humans exchange breath with trees and plants. Science is bringing us back to an appreciation of some wisdom that we, in Western culture at least, seem to have forgotten: that we cannot breathe, we cannot exist without participating in a cooperative effort with the rest of creation. At its base, everything that exists is part of a dynamic, cooperative, unified whole.

The recognition of that unity is not new. It is an ancient wisdom that was once basic to the formation of whole cultures among Eastern peoples and Native tribes, whose lives kept them in close contact with Earth's own processes. Every day they could see how things related to each other, and were careful not to disrupt them. That is no longer the case. Living in cities, we rarely even touch the earth that gives us our food; we don't walk—we ride! Instead of cooperating, we compete: who has the biggest, the best, the most? We begin to believe that we function independently, detached from each other, detached from the rest of creation. Our culture encourages us to seek (but never to find) our identity and our value in what we have. Our consumerist culture has forgotten about the importance, the inevitability, of *connections*.

When we ignore the connections, life systems break down. That is what is happening: our contemporary ecological and societal deterioration is the warning signal. Our planetary survival may depend upon our ability to recover our awareness of the Oneness that undergirds the whole of creation.

The Oneness of all that is has been celebrated by great poets and artists throughout the ages, and it is bedrock teaching in religious traditions. In popular (or mainstream) Christianity, that teaching is most often only a muted voice, yet the mystical tradition in Christianity, as well as that of many of the world's religions, has carried consistent witness to the fact that, at the deepest level, all things are one, united in their Source. Each tradition has its own way of approaching that Oneness, sometimes through meditation or prayer practices, sometimes through compassionate, selfless service. The mystical traditions hold out to us the promise that this unity lies at the very core of our identity and wants to draw us, through our life experience, to realize our true destiny.

How wonderful that, just when we need it, science produces its own evidence of such a Oneness. The availability of intercultural communication has made it possible for us to become familiar and to learn from the many other religious traditions that have been providing wisdom for people over the course of ages. Such dialogue confirms—if we needed confirmation—the universality and truth of humanity's fragmented but persistent groping toward unity, and emphasizes both the urgency as well as the opportunity of the present moment. We can recognize, in our own historical experience, the presence and the inspiration of the Spirit of God nudging all people to respond to God's intent to draw us into the realization of this holy unity.

Three Lenses

We want now to proceed to sketch, in broad terms, the dimensions of this unity, understanding that we must always be looking through three lenses, which in the end converge into a single vision. The first is the lens of science. The second is that of humanity's solidarity as a species, and the third is the deepest spiritual lens: the vision of communion. Our task is to honor what we see through each of these lenses and, finally, to integrate them.

Science, the first lens, may well be a microscope or a telescope! We see that, at every level from microscopically tiny to cosmically expansive, the whole creation is actually engaged in continuing re-creation. It is always breaking down and breaking through to unite in new forms, on micro as well as macro levels. The process involves continual cooperation, mutuality, and exchange. We see evidence of this process in the attraction of molecules for each other, continually exchanging and changing, uniting, separating, uniting in a new combination to form a new entity.

If we take time to reflect upon nature's cycles and seasons of growth and decay, if we think about the exchange between trees and humans that is involved in every breath we draw, we can recognize the phenomenon of universal interdependence. If we look closely, we recognize that everything lives in reciprocity; we see it in the way plants and bugs are always interacting, in the fact that all species provide food for each other. When we hear birds singing, when we see mating, when we experience human affection and love, we are participating in a great, continuous process of exchange. We see it finally in the fact that death in living things gives way to new life. At least metaphorically, everything is always both eating and being eaten, wounding and being wounded. The pattern of the cycle—life/death/life—is familiar, but it is never merely banal repetition. Something genuinely new is always emerging: a continual, ongoing new creation.

As a principle, we can say that in fact, everything comes to be, *everything exists only by sharing its energy*, sharing its life, always groping toward a new unity. That is the first lens, the lens of science and reason.

Through the second lens—humanity's solidarity—we see the same phenomenon expressed in a different mode. We see humans in their personal, social, and economic relationships with each other, or with other species, and we speak of *solidarity*: a sense of being with, caring for, sharing (of resources, education, and medicine, for instance) that has an eye to justice, equality, respect for dignity, and integrity. We see conscious collaboration for the good of the whole.[4] This lens can also detect the disparities, the inequities, the fragmentation; it will see the violations of unity.

In our new perception of planetary interconnection, solidarity involves awareness not only of the responsibilities for care in interpersonal relationships, but also a much more critical and extensive alertness to the power of systems: how do social, political, and economic systems (local, national, and global) interact to cause or to perpetuate situations of inequity, discrimination, and poverty? What are the connections, for instance, between economic exploitation and the degradation of the planet; between extravagant wealth and overconsumption in some places, and poverty and starvation in others? Solidarity means presence to and with those who are oppressed, joining in protest and resistance (breaking down), and it means joining in creative efforts to establish new, more just and collaborative patterns (re-formation). The lens of solidarity can spur us to action.

Finally, the third lens is a vision of the totality. It is the experience of the fundamental Holy Oneness that is recognized in the mystical traditions as God, Divine, the Source of all that is. Here we speak of *communion*. The first two lenses are each limited. At the outset, objective observation of the processes that undergird the working of the universe ordinarily addresses itself primarily to the mind, the head. But such observation can open, through the human capacity for awe and wonder, into a vision of Holy Oneness. The sense of solidarity also may involve both head and heart. It too can open into an all-encompassing sense of love and compassion for the whole of humanity. Both of these lenses contribute to the opening of the third, the transcendent experience of the Holy Oneness of all that is, which catches up the whole person into an experience of total transformation. The Sacred infuses everything that is, and each lens is a holy pathway. It is the mystical lens of communion that most deeply and truly reveals the nature of human destiny as moving toward the Source, toward unity with all that is, toward union in and with God.

This third lens unifies the other two in their Divine Ground. We can understand, from the inside as it were, the obvious necessity for humans to align themselves with the fundamental Earth processes of sharing, and choose to order our lives in solidarity with the needy and oppressed to advance the cause of unity. The three lenses together reveal to us the ultimate reality of genuine "right relations," which is the meaning of justice. To be in right relation with the rest of creation is the graced task of every human being, and the destiny of humanity as a whole. In this text we explore the interplay of these lenses in the development of a spirituality of justice at this time in our history.

Thinking globally, imagining our human identity as completely relational: to imagine this way makes the frame very wide, and we risk becoming simply flat and superficial. If our frame becomes wider, we must, equivalently, go deeper. We can't expect real answers to justice questions to come from the market. The market always deals with "resources" rather than "relatives." And we can't expect technology, or simple "information," helpful though it is, to save us. The real vision, and most especially the needed *wisdom*, comes from our tapping into the Oneness at its Source.

So now we need to ask: What does this vision require of us at this moment in history? What does our own Christian tradition contribute to this vision of unity? How do we move from knowing with our heads to the deep, steady, passionate engagement of our hearts and our lives? How can this understanding be brought to bear in our intent to follow, as faithfully as we can, the gospel of Jesus, to participate most fully in this movement toward realization of Christ's prayer "that all may be one"?

We turn now to try to ground our spirituality of justice in the wisdom of the Judaic and Christian faith traditions. Obviously this brief overview is limited in its presentation. To understand and to live in fidelity to our tradition are the tasks of a lifetime.

Chapter Two

God's Hope for Solidarity:
The Hebrew Scriptures

The Lord said to Israel:
"The relation between yourselves and me
is always that of strangers and settlers.
If you will live in the world like strangers,
remembering that you are here but temporarily,
then I your God will be a settler in your midst
in that my Presence will dwell with you permanently.
But if you will regard yourselves as settlers,
as permanent owners of the land on which you live,
when the land is actually not yours but mine,
my Presence will be a stranger,
in that it will not dwell in your midst.
In any case, you, O Israel, you and I
cannot be strangers and settlers at the same time.
If you act the stranger, I will be the settler,
and if you act the settler, I must be the stranger.

Rabbi Mark Tannenbaum[5]

It is almost impossible to read the Hebrew scriptures with-out noticing that there are two very different stories, each speaking of the origin of creation and human life. The first, in Genesis 1, portrays God, Yahweh, creating by the divine word everything that is. At the end of each day, we are told that "God saw that it was good." On the sixth day, God created man and woman in the divine image, and endowed them, as God's image, with responsibility to relate to the creation in his stead.[6] At the end of that day, "God saw everything that he had made, and indeed, it was very good." And on the seventh day, God rested, and blessed and hallowed that day as a day of rest.⁷

That original "goodness," blessed by God at the end of every phase of divine creativity, would always shine through the creation to draw the hearts and minds of humans to celebrate the wonder of this creative God. "The heavens are telling the glory of God; and the firmament proclaims [God's] handiwork," sings the psalmist, thrilling at the fact that, through all the earth, the whole of creation continuously announces the magnificence and mystery of its Creator (Ps. 19). "O Lord, how manifold are your works!" the psalmist meditates. "In wisdom you have made them all." And God continues to provide for the self-renewal of all life forms: "When you send forth your spirit they are created; and you renew the face of the ground" (Ps. 104:24–30). The beauty, the fecundity, and the prodigality of nature were and are an awesome gift, continually awakening joy and grateful celebration of the Creator's goodness, overflowing in song and dance and artistry.

A second account of creation (Gen. 2–3) pictures the original human formed by God from the dust of the earth, surrounded by a beautiful garden. Here the biblical writer gives an account of how the original goodness and order of creation were disrupted when the first humans succumbed to the temptation to "want to be like God." What ensued was trouble, and in subsequent chapters and generations we see human beings acting in ways that are hostile, hurtful, and violent toward each other. By the time of Noah, in chapter 6, "the earth was filled with violence" (Gen. 6:11). God determined to start over, flooded the earth, and initiated a new beginning, making a covenant, this time not just with humans but with the whole earth community. God emphatically reiterates that this covenant includes every species, "every living creature of all flesh that is on the earth" (Gen. 9:16). So Noah, his family, and one pair of every species are saved from the flood. Humans once again spread across the earth and settle in. At this time, "the whole earth had one language and the same words" (Gen. 11:1).

But now humans had learned to make bricks and decided to build themselves "a city and a tower with its top in the heavens," in order "to make a name for ourselves" (11:4). It was, perhaps, a final prideful attempt to lay claim to the power of God. Seeing that humans were once again on the wrong track, God dispersed them and confused their languages before they could do any more damage. Now they would no longer be readily able to communicate with each other; they would henceforth experience themselves as separate, unrelated strangers to one another. Unity shattered into diversity.

And so the essential goodness and unity of creation—coming, as it did, from the word and the hand of God—have been disrupted by human beings. But still God does not give up. The story of the tower of Babel is the turning point of the Genesis narrative: God would now try a different approach.

In chapter 12, the biblical writer recounts God's call to Abram, Israel's ancestor. Thus begins the long story of God's involvement with the people of Israel. God once again starts over, as it were, in the hope of creating a particular human community that can serve as a genuine model for humanity.[8]

In summary fashion, we might say that in the Hebrew scriptures God reveals the divine identity in two "names" which are key to Israel's understanding not only of God, but also of Israel's own identity in relation to God. In a first self-identification, God says to Moses, "I am the God of your father, the God of Abraham, the God of Isaac, and the God of

Jacob" (Ex. 3:6). And, God continues, "I have observed the misery of my people who are in Egypt. . . . I have heard their cry on account of their taskmasters. Indeed, I know their sufferings, and I have come down to deliver them . . ." (Ex. 3:7–8). Though limited by patriarchal presumptions, this naming reveals some important dimensions of God's nature. God is not attached to place or to cultic ritual, but rather to persons. Further, God's interest is not only in individual persons but, as Israel's subsequent history testifies, God is one who cares about the condition of suffering humanity.

Something in the human cry of distress evokes a response of action-to-save from this God. Israel, from its very beginnings, would know their God as one whose heart is moved by human suffering, one who is ready and willing to act with their cooperation, to inspire, to encourage and support the human desire for liberation. Israel was born out of the experience of being liberated by God from slavery in Egypt. The exodus experience and the covenant with God in the desert were never simply past events. They contained, for Israel, the kernel of Israel's ever-present understanding not just of God but of its own historical purpose. Israel's experience of God was inseparably religious, political, and communal, and so its covenant with this God committed both parties to a continual engagement in the historical process of human liberation. God would be partner in Israel's history, promising empowerment to move from the confinement of slavery, brokenness, and oppression into the open space of freedom. Such is the promise of Israel's God, and of Israel's faith.

Encoded in the deliverance from Egypt was the message that Israel was called to embody a society whose sense of justice runs so deep that it could not allow tyranny, oppression, or poverty to exist in its midst. Because, in this founding event, it was not by trusting military might but by trusting the power of God that Israel was liberated, it would forever be challenged to break the hold of those idols of violence and war as means to peace. Israel's social structure was to be a model that brings hope to humankind, to embody a new vision for human society.

Even though God seemed to single out Israel as special, God was in no way an easy mark, subject to manipulation. For this same God also presents a second self-identification. Appearing to Moses in a bush that is burning but not consumed, the Holy One reveals to him the divine name, "I AM WHO I AM" (Ex. 3:14). This open-ended, nondefining, unfathomable phrase left generations to come wrestling with awed awareness of the essential mystery and incomprehensibility that surround the Holy One. This God would tolerate no second-guessing of the divine intent, no covering of bases: this God adamantly refuses to be associated with any other gods.

Still, this same mysteriously named God engages Moses to undertake the difficult task of confronting Pharaoh with his oppression of the Israelites, and then to suffer through their backsliding and bellyaching in the desert. Humans would come to know God both through encounters with God's creation (as did Moses with the burning bush) and through the longings of their own hearts for freedom and wholeness. God is present to the cry of suffering slaves, and that presence manifests itself in wondrous deeds, such as the plagues and the parting of the sea that enabled the Israelites to escape from Egypt. God also guides Israel's history in a more personal fashion, selecting particular individuals at particular times for particular missions: Moses, David, the prophets.

Israel's historical task is to live with the tension of a God who is characterized equally by transcendent, holy mystery, and by personal involvement in Israel's journey to freedom.

God reminds the people throughout their history that they know from their own experience in Egypt what it is like to be needy, to be enslaved and powerless, to be an outsider, an alien and wandering homeless in the desert. They know that this God, with whom they have made covenant, is deeply concerned with people's freedom and well-being. If such compassionate solidarity is characteristic of Israel's God and if they are God's people, then their way of living must be patterned upon what they have learned of God. Their social relationships must exhibit care and concern for others who are powerless or in need. This concern extends even to strangers and outsiders: "The alien [stranger] who resides with you shall be to you as the citizen [native] among you; you shall love the alien as yourself" (Lev. 19:34). Even more strongly, God insists, "You shall not oppress a resident alien. You know the heart of an alien [stranger] for you were aliens in the land of Egypt" (Ex. 23:9).

"You *know the heart* of the stranger," and you shall love that heart as your own. The covenant with God requires that they remember their own experience and their aspirations. Their own hearts' memory must join them in compassion with any who suffer. The people of Israel must not only reverence their God, but the depth and authenticity of their relationship with God takes its measure from how they themselves care for the needy in their midst, whether they be "their own kind" or different from them. The compassionate solidarity of this covenanted people is to witness to God's hope for unity among a diverse and scattered humanity.[9]

That covenant solidarity extends even to the land. Sabbath

is to be observed every seventh day; on that day the land as well as the people will rest from labor. Every seventh year will be observed as a sabbatical year: debts will be remitted, slaves freed, and the land will lie fallow to rest from its labors (Dt. 15:1–18; Lev. 25). Whatever produce there is will be shared with whoever is in need. And after seven times seven years, a jubilee year will be declared. At this time "you shall proclaim liberty throughout the land" (Lev. 25:10): land would then be returned to its original inhabitants. "The land shall not be sold in perpetuity, for the land is mine; with me you are but aliens and tenants," says God (Lev. 25:23). Before God, even Israel is a "stranger" alongside every other human with no rights of possession.

Just as Israel belongs to God, so does the land. The importance of sabbath for ordering priorities is not simply a theoretical ideal but is a practical, structural part of Israel's social life. Work can never become an idol; land can never become a possession. Restorative justice is the guiding principle of Israel's morality.

The land shares in the covenant in an even deeper way. Two passages from the prophets illustrate the relationship quite graphically. The prophet Isaiah perceives a causal connection between covenant fidelity and the flourishing of the land:

> The earth dries up and withers,
>> the world languishes and withers;
>> the heavens languish together with the earth.
> The earth lies polluted
>> under its inhabitants;
> for they have transgressed laws,
>> violated the statutes,
>> broken the everlasting covenant.
> Therefore a curse devours the earth,

and its inhabitants suffer for their guilt;
therefore the inhabitants of the earth dwindled,
and few people are left.

(Is. 24:4–6)

Hosea makes the same connection:

There is no faithfulness or loyalty,
    and no knowledge of God in the land.
Swearing, lying, and murder,
    and stealing and adultery break out;
    bloodshed follows bloodshed.
Therefore the land mourns,
    and all who live in it languish;
together with the wild animals
    and the birds of the air,
    even the fish of the sea are perishing.

(Hos. 4:1–3)

When people neglect justice, the land also suffers. Hosea is making a further striking connection: if people really know God, he says, covenant justice and the well-being of the land will follow. Conversely, when there is injustice or abuse of the land, the people are out of touch with God. Failure in one area is symptomatic of failure in the other two. It is all of a piece: religion cannot be separated from people's relations with each other, and with the land. The goodness of the One God permeates the whole. The human task, in centuries of trial and error, is to learn what it means to live in right relation. Israel is to provide an example, but the task would eventually be seen to belong to all the nations of the world.

The prophets, as God's spokespersons, condemn Israel's failures and misperceptions. But they also hold out the promise that a return to covenant fidelity, with each other and with the land, will restore Israel's intimacy with God:

> I will make for you a covenant . . . with the wild animals, the
> birds of the air, and the creeping things of the ground; and I will
> abolish the bow, the sword, and war from the land; and I will
> make you lie down in safety. . . . I will take you for my wife in
> faithfulness; and you shall know the Lord.
>
> (Hos. 2:18, 20)

The effect of covenant solidarity—or its lack—extends to the whole creation. God, the people, and the land are intended to be in peaceful "right relationship" with each other.

In summary, Israel's God is at once an awesome nameless Mystery and intimately involved with the well-being of the whole creation. God has compassion for people's suffering and an active concern for justice, understood not in terms of keeping laws in order to maintain a status quo, but rather as intervening to protect the needy and powerless from oppression. How people relate to each other is how they relate to God, and both are implicated in the well-being of the land. God's concern is for the whole creation, integrally related in a three-dimensional reciprocal process.

God's covenant with Israel is a covenant of mutuality. When the people of Israel truly "know God," they will most faithfully embody God's own characteristic compassion and justice in their relationship with each other and with the land, and God will be deeply and consistently present in their midst. This was, clearly, to be a different kind of people, holy as God is holy, favored as God's people only because and insofar as their collective life identified them as a people consecrated to God in an ethos of compassion, justice, and holiness.

But as years passed into centuries, the people of Israel over and over again let themselves be lured into imitating the ways of other nations. They initiated a monarchy, a move that was viewed both positively and negatively in the tradition. The role of king was to govern in God's stead, as God would govern; the nation was a theocracy, and the king was leader in both the secular and religious spheres. The king would exemplify and administer the covenant ethos. As described in Psalm 72, he would judge the people with righteousness and the poor with justice; he would give deliverance to the needy and redeem their lives from oppression and violence.

There were periods when Israel prospered and knew God's blessing of shalom. There were kings, evaluated chiefly in terms of their fidelity to the worship of the One God, who "did what was right in the sight of the Lord" (e.g., 1 Kgs. 15:11). But there was also a series of kings whose reign is identified cryptically: "he did what was evil in the sight of the Lord" (cf. 1 Kgs. 16:25). There were times when an errant king heeded the warning of a prophet and turned back to covenant fidelity (cf. 2 Chr. 15). Nevertheless, Israel seemed to have a problem with recurrent amnesia: they forgot their own story. Those in power were vulnerable to coveting the lifestyle of the other nations, as if wealth and luxury, armies and military prowess were Israel's source of identity and security. In the tenth century BCE, the kingdom fractured into two opposing royalties, Israel and Judah henceforth engaging in tribal warfare, kin against kin.

Through the centuries, bribes, cheating, and fraud would become rampant in the practice of business. The class lines separating rich from poor became hardened. "Ownership" of land became concentrated in the hands of a wealthy elite. The social systems themselves were causing suffering and oppression. It was a scenario like that of Israel's early history in Egypt, but with role reversals: Israel's wealthy elite was now playing the role that Pharaoh had played, and its own people were once again in bondage.

In their internal patterns of ruling, the leaders in the society neglected their primary responsibility to administer justice to their own people. "The Lord enters into judgment with the elders and princes of his people," says Isaiah. "It is you who have devoured the vineyard; the spoil of the poor is in your houses. What do you mean by crushing my people, by grinding the face of the poor? says the Lord God of hosts" (Is. 3:14–15).

And the kings were consistently putting their trust not in God but in their own clever schemes, their treaties, their own power to do battle, which was not what God had in mind. God's presence made itself felt through the often stinging and unwelcome words of prophets, recalling Israel to its true identity as a covenant people.

The life of the prophet Jeremiah typifies the role of the prophet. Toward the end of the seventh century BCE, the powerful Babylonians threatened to invade the land of Judah. God's instruction, spoken through Jeremiah, was that King Zedekiah should not try to resist, but should submit to the power of Babylon (21:8–9). Jeremiah even acted out Israel's captivity, putting a yoke on himself to symbolize the yoke of the Babylonians to which they would have to submit if they were to survive (27:1–13). Jeremiah forecast death and destruction if the king sought to defend his country by means of arms. God, he said, would be fighting on the side of the Babylonians this time! Surprisingly, Jeremiah speaks of Nebuchadnezzar, the king of Babylon, as the instrument of God's will in this historic moment (27:6–8), just as later on, Isaiah would speak of King Cyrus of Persia as "God's anointed" (Is. 45:1). When the people are in fact exiled in Babylon, Jeremiah counsels them, as God intends, to "seek the welfare of the city where I have sent you into exile, and pray to the Lord on its behalf." This is how they will find their own peace (29:7).

Still, while the Babylonians are at the gate, Jeremiah, directed by God, holds up the hope for the future. From the prison where he was being held for speaking against the king, Jeremiah buys a piece of property at Anathoth, in witness of God's pledge to restore the land to Israel (32:1–15). The covenant would endure; God would simply wait for the people to recover their senses (cf. also 29:10).

But what a reversal! Evidently, Israel was not God's only interest on the historical scene. "God was more the champion of justice than the champion of Israel."[10] God's history of working "wondrous deeds" on behalf of this people could not be presumed upon to protect and maintain the power of the king and the state; clearly, God was unwilling to sacrifice the lives of the people on the altar of national pride. Shoring up empire was not on God's agenda, nor had a powerful military any part to play in God's way of doing things. Quite the contrary: God would have to teach Israel the lesson that such pretense of independent self-sufficiency was completely contrary to the terms and the spirit of the covenant. They would find peace in making peace.

Israel's apostasy from the covenant had a deep impact upon the authenticity of the nation's worship. True, the people were dutifully performing all the rituals, and they were fasting and sacrificing for all they were worth. But the injustice, oppression, violence, and greed in Israel's society was all the evidence God needed to recognize that their ritual performances were tantamount to idolatry: they no longer "knew God." God was sick and tired of the people's pretense (Is. 1:10–15). In God's eyes, they were an adulterous people (Hos. 2:1ff.), hon-

oring God with their lips but not their hearts (Is. 29:13).
Jeremiah protests:

> Amend your ways and your doings, and let me dwell with you
> in this place. Do not trust in these deceptive words: "This is
> the temple of the Lord, the temple of the Lord, the temple of
> the Lord." For if you truly amend your ways and your doings,
> if you truly act justly one with another, if you do not oppress
> the alien, the orphan, and the widow, or shed innocent blood
> in this place, and if you do not go after other gods to your own
> hurt, then I will dwell with you in this place. . . .
>
> (Jer. 7:3–7)

Consistently through centuries of their history, prophets
faithfully denounced the infidelity and reminded both kings
and people of their responsibility to their covenant relationship with God. As if with a single voice, they tried to open the
people's eyes to the incompatibility of worship with the existence of greed and injustice in their midst. Amos spoke for
God: "I hate, I despise your festivals. . . . But let justice roll
down like waters and righteousness like an ever-flowing
stream" (5:21, 24).

In one of the most trenchant of the prophetic pronouncements, Isaiah announces God's judgment on Israel's religious
practice:

> Look, you serve your own interest on your fast day,
>   and oppress all your workers.
> Look, you fast only to quarrel and to fight
>   and to strike with a wicked fist.
> Such fasting as you do today
>   will not make your voice heard on high. . . .
> Is not this the fast that I choose:
>   to loose the bonds of injustice,
>   to undo the thongs of the yoke,

> to let the oppressed go free,
>> and to break every yoke?
> Is it not to share your bread with the hungry,
>> and bring the homeless poor into your house;
>> when you see the naked, to cover them,
>> and not to hide yourself from your own kin?
>
> (Is. 58:3–4, 6–7)

Another prophet, Micah, cut through the multitude of their vain religious practices and went immediately to the core of what is essential (cf. Mic. 6). Placed in context of a "hearing," God reminds the people of a history full of saving acts. The prophet turns over in his mind the possible sacrifices he might offer: burnt offerings of calves, or rams with ten thousand rivers of oil, or even his own son? God, in turn, recounts Israel's infidelities: wicked scales, a bag of dishonest weights, the violence of the wealthy, the lies and deceit of the people, their idolatrous practice. Sacrifice and rituals are worthless.

Micah sums up in a few words all that is necessary: "[God] has told you, O mortal, what is good; and what does the Lord require of you but to do justice, and to love kindness, and to walk humbly with your God?" Worship of this God has everything to do with how one *lives*. At the heart of Israel's relationship with God is no complicated program or performance. The covenant is utterly rooted in "right relations."

Nevertheless, even when Israel strayed from fidelity, God never for a moment forgot the covenant: "Surely I know the plans I have for you . . . plans for your welfare and not for harm, to give you a future with hope. Then . . . when you search for me, you will find me; if you seek me with all your heart, I will let you find me, says the Lord" (Jer. 29:10–14). God longs for their hearts to return to the ways of the covenant, and even speaks of a new covenant, different and more interior than the old one: "It will not be like the covenant that I made with their ancestors when I took them by the hand to bring them out of the land of Egypt. . . . But this is the covenant that I will make . . . : I will put my law within them, and I will write it on their hearts . . ." (Jer. 31:32–33). God longs to be with humans from the inside out.

Finally, some prophets caught glimpses of an inclusive vision of a world characterized by righteousness and peace encompassing all peoples, the land, the whole of creation. Ezekiel prophesied a time of idyllic harmony, when the land would yield plentiful blessing and the people would dwell without fear, in safety and complete peace (34:25–29). Isaiah envisioned a day when all nations would stream to Jerusalem to be instructed in the ways of God. Then

> [God] shall judge between the nations,
>   and shall arbitrate for many peoples;
> they shall beat their swords into plowshares,
>   and their spears into pruning hooks;
> nation shall not lift up sword against nation,
>   neither shall they learn war any more.
>   (2:1–4)

And then,

> The wolf shall live with the lamb,
>   the leopard shall lie down with the kid. . . .
> They will not hurt or destroy
>   on all my holy mountain;
> for the earth will be full of the knowledge of the Lord
>   as the waters cover the sea.
>   (11:6–9)

The book of Isaiah also contains five startling and much-discussed oracles that seem to move in the direction of a very broad and inclusive sense of universality (19:16–25).[11] In the last three of these oracles, the prophet speaks first of a time—"on that day"—when apparently after painful conquest, there would be "an altar to the Lord in the center of the land of Egypt, and a pillar to the Lord at its border." The text probably refers to the presence of worshiping diaspora Jews in Egypt, and perhaps also to proselytes. But it goes on to foretell, in language reminiscent of Israel's own exodus journey, that God would act on behalf of the Egyptians (19:19–22), conveying the sense that Israel is not the only nation under God's care.

In the next oracle, Isaiah prophesies that "there will be a highway from Egypt to Assyria, and the Assyrian will come into Egypt, and the Egyptian into Assyria, and the Egyptians will worship with the Assyrians" (19:23). And finally,

> On that day Israel will be the third with Egypt and Assyria, a blessing in the midst of the earth, whom the Lord of hosts has blessed, saying, "Blessed be Egypt my people, and Assyria the work of my hands, and Israel my heritage."
>
> (19:24–25)

Do these lines indicate movement, in Israel's prophetic tradition, from religious imperialism to religious pluralism? The text itself seems to move from images of conquest, to open communication, to worship that unites the various peoples—in their diversity—as one people of God. The text does not speak of Israel in Egypt. Egypt was to be Egypt, not Israel; the Assyrians were to worship God as Assyrians. In the final oracle, Isaiah seems to hold up a vision of a time when present enemies—the three largest nations central to the known world of the time—would worship together, each nation, unique and individual, precious to Israel's God and each one a blessing to the whole earth in their worship of God.

Can *we* imagine such a thing? God's hope, expressed in the Hebrew scriptures (and especially in the prophetic tradition), is that the people of Israel, in covenant with God, would be a light to the nations. Their polity and their community of compassion, justice, and peace would set an example through which the people of many nations could join Israel in worshiping and in living according to the ways of God. Such prophecy called the people to reimagine their world. It reminded them that human vision can become dull and shortsighted; it can begin to settle for a status quo that takes war for granted and assumes that, naturally, some may thrive at the expense of the rest. God's covenant solidarity rests upon Israel's cooperation in giving living witness to divine compassion and justice. The prophets were calling the people to keep alive God's hope for a better world, in which right relations would issue in peace for everyone, for the whole creation. They were reminding the people of their responsibility to act that hope into reality.

Chapter Three

Communion:
The Way of Jesus

Unless a grain of wheat falls into the earth and dies, it remains just a single grain; but if it dies, it bears much fruit.

Jn. 12:24

Centuries passed, and in the fullness of time, Mary, pregnant with the life of the messiah, greets her cousin Elizabeth with a joyous and revolutionary song.[12] She praises the God of her people, who is manifesting anew, now in her own experience, the "wondrous deeds" that have been carried in Israel's memory through the centuries. Mary is, first of all, a woman; she is a member of an oppressed Palestinian society; she is young, uneducated, a peasant, unmarried, and pregnant. Certainly she can claim no entitlement whatsoever to be the bearer of the messiah, yet God "has looked with favor on the lowliness of his servant" (Lk. 1:48). God's initiative, God's graciousness, is at the center of Mary's joy.

Her song goes on to celebrate the coming of a new age: a time when God's mighty arm will once again show itself on behalf of the lowly, the hungry, and the poor, and reverse the accepted economic and social order that has favored the powerful and the wealthy. God's choice of this particular woman to be mother of the messiah portends a social order that manifests a compassionate and unprecedented reversal of the rules: God will "scatter," "bring down," and "send away empty" those who have power and wealth; God will "exalt" the lowly, those who are poor and hungry. The words are strong prophecy, and they promise a shockingly concrete transformation of society and its hierarchies.

Apart from the story, told only in Luke's Gospel, of Jesus' surprise visit to the temple (Lk. 2:41–51), we know nothing about Jesus' youth or young adulthood. In all four Gospels, Jesus' first public appearance was in the context of his baptism by John. The narrative in Mark's Gospel, the earliest of the Gospels, tells the story quite simply. At a moment when Jesus was submitting himself to baptism by John, Jesus "saw the heavens torn apart and the Spirit descending like a dove on him. And a voice came from heaven, 'You are my Son, the Beloved; with you I am well pleased'" (Mk. 1:9–11).

Though the accounts of Jesus' baptism as narrated by Matthew and Luke seem to suggest that this experience was objectively visible and audible to onlookers, Mark's account focuses on the subjective experience of Jesus himself; "he saw the heavens torn apart," and the voice from heaven is addressed to Jesus: "You are my Son . . ." (Mk. 1:10–11). Some powerful new awareness of God's personal intimacy and involvement in his life was awakened in Jesus, such that he would know himself in relation to God as son to father. It was an experience of communion with God that could not be contained. It propelled Jesus to preach and teach and heal. He needed to share what he knew with everyone. The important point for us is that from the beginning, Jesus' ministry is grounded in an experience of intimacy and communion with God.

All three of the synoptic Gospels relate that immediately following this experience, Jesus retreated into the desert (Mk. 1:12–13; Mt. 4:1–11; Lk. 4:1–13). No doubt, following such a powerful experience, Jesus would have felt compelled to sort things out, to "process" the experience, to try to discern what it meant for his life and how he could be faithful to its content. How was he going to live out that calling? What would be his next step?

Another level of meaning may reside in the Gospels. This sojourn in the desert is placed at the beginning of Jesus' ministry. All three episodes that Matthew and Luke recount as temptations by Satan relate to a skewed or self-serving use of power: to turn stones into bread, to jump off the pinnacle of the temple, and to accept all the glory and authority of all the kingdoms of the world, which, Satan says quite bluntly, "has been given over to me" (Lk. 4:6). We tend to read the "temptation narrative" as if right from the start Jesus got it all straight: he resisted Satan's lure and came out of the desert clean and clear to pursue his God-given mission without further trouble.

But perhaps not. Perhaps the placing of those temptations at the beginning of the Gospels is programmatic, a way of saying that throughout his life, power and its use would be an area that would require Jesus' continued self-scrutiny and renunciation. His life was given to revealing the reign of God and the power of God. That could only be accomplished step by step, in the demands of each day. It would inevitably involve confrontation: with the power of the Roman Empire oppressing the Jewish people and, more particularly, with the power of the Jewish religious establishment. The former laid heavy taxes upon already stressed populations; the latter oppressed them with their cult of the temple and with the innumerable dos and don'ts that made God's law a source of bondage rather than freedom. Jesus would have to take stands, assess the consequences, and hold himself faithful to the path that emerged as he began teaching and healing.

Would he be seduced by the image of the messiah that the public expected—a political leader, a powerful king who would secure the freedom of the Jewish nation? Would he have the courage needed to confront the Jewish leaders with a threateningly different interpretation of what it means to live the covenant faith? Or would he be overwhelmed and back down? What if his own life were at risk? Finally, would his ego lay claim to "specialness" because of this gift of newly awakened awareness of God's intimacy and the power that accompanied it? Would he get high on this power and use it to enhance his own comfort, popularity, and status?

To pose questions in this way is to underscore the fact that factors both external and internal need continual discernment. Public confrontations with established authorities, questions of collective expectation, the public image, conforming his behavior to what he thinks the people want of him: these temptations seem to come from the external world. Internally, these same issues take the form of self-aggrandizement and ego enhancement, using things and people to serve his own ends, to make himself look or feel good.

These temptations were subtle. They were not temptations to do anything patently evil. In fact, one could assume that the power to turn stones into bread would be a *good*: think how many people could be fed! Or the challenge to accept all the power of the kingdoms of the world: surely Jesus could have done enormous good for people if he had been willing to accept a position of power. But taking this direction would risk changing the focus and purpose of his ministry. "God's reign" required a very different approach.

Jesus could not likely have dealt with these issues once and for all in the desert. Rather, he would have to deal with these temptations throughout his ministry. From what fundamental attitude would his choices spring? Would he be able to keep his motivations clear? The Gospel writers present them at the beginning of the Gospels so that we can keep in mind the fundamental attitude that was at stake for Jesus each step of the way.

We note that at each challenge of the tempter, Jesus responds with a quotation from scripture, a quotation that helps him position himself squarely in his commitment to do God's will in faithful obedience, at whatever cost to himself. What the scene tells us is that Jesus, as a faithful Jew, had deeply pondered the scriptures of the Jewish people, and had been formed in his attitudes by studying and praying those scriptures. When he came to a crisis, then, those scriptures provided the attitudes that would allow him to discern God's way for him in the difficult choices that would face him.

For Jesus, dealing with issues of power—his own power and the "powers that be"—would be critical to his ministry. He would require times alone, times of intense prayer to stay in touch with that wellspring of Divine Life that had opened within him. Living out of a deep sense of intimacy and communion with God had to be the continuous grounding impulse for his active life.

Jesus returned from the desert "filled with the power of the Spirit" (Lk. 4:14). He began preaching *metanoia*: not just repentance but a complete revolution of people's minds and hearts.

Israel's prophetic tradition comes into new focus when Jesus, inaugurating his ministry in Luke's Gospel, reads in the synagogue from the scroll of Isaiah and announces the initiation of a *kairos,* a special time. Today, he says, is a new beginning: today begins a time of jubilee that opens a new era, as Isaiah prophesied:

The Spirit of the Lord is upon me,
because he has anointed me to bring good news to the poor.
He has sent me to proclaim release to the captives,
and recovery of sight to the blind,
to let the oppressed go free,
to proclaim the year of the Lord's favor.

(Lk. 4:17–19)

For Luke's Gospel, then, the year of Jubilee—the year when debts are cancelled, slaves are freed, and all things are returned to their original right relationship with God—is the framework of meaning for Jesus' ministry. And so he begins to preach and to enact the restorative justice of jubilee, teaching and healing, calling others, one by one, to be with him as disciples. At a time when Israel was once again in bondage, this time to the Roman Empire, Jesus gathers around him a band of ordinary folks and tries, during his brief ministry, to awaken them—and anyone who would listen—to a new summons to covenant fidelity. He speaks of "the reign of God" and tries with his storytelling and his healing to help people imagine what their world could be like if God were in charge.

His message does not involve organizing armies and overthrowing governments. In fact, he shows little interest in conventional organizational issues of state power. Instead, in the tradition of Israel's prophets, Jesus' eyes are on the poor and the marginalized and on the laws and structures that keep them so.

He warns the wealthy of the danger of trying to "serve two masters" and of the futility of trying to store up riches (Mt. 6:24, 19–21). Instead, he urges them to share what they have with the poor, to see the helpless and the needy in their midst with eyes of justice and compassion. He reminds the people, as did the prophets before him, that it is mercy that God loves, not sacrifice (Mt. 9:13), and he challenges them to love everyone, even their enemies. They should love as God loves, impartially making "the sun rise on the evil and on the good," and sending "rain on the righteous and on the unrighteous" (Mt. 5:44–45). In place of vengeance, Jesus suggests highly creative, nonviolent responses to wrongdoing, like turning the other cheek or going the extra mile (Mt. 5:38–42).[13]

They must forgive anyone who has hurt them, not seven but seventy-seven times—that is, you can't ever stop (Mt. 18:21)! They shouldn't invite their friends to their parties because their friends will repay them (Lk. 14:14)! His stories puzzle and confuse the powerful, turning their values upside down: the last will be first, and the one who wants to be great must become the servant; the humble will be exalted and the exalted humbled. "The least among all of you is the greatest," he tells them (Lk. 9:48). He proclaims, as Mary his mother had prophesied, that values would be reversed, that the kingdom of God belongs to the poor, that the hungry will be filled and the rich go hungry, that sorrow will be turned into joy and joy into sorrow (Lk. 6:20ff.). His paradoxes are outrageous and upsetting, challenging assumptions, questioning priorities.

His compassion and zeal can scarcely be contained. He quickly begins restoring health and life wherever he sees it wanting and wherever he finds an open and receptive heart. The blind are given sight and the deaf hearing; demons are expelled, the paralyzed are enabled to move, the withered and the bent over are smoothed and straightened. Jesus cannot be limited by separatist restrictions of the holiness laws: his touch heals a leper and a hemorrhaging woman; he eats with taxpayers and sinners. He claims to forgive sins and proposes radical reinterpretation of the sabbath proscriptions and the laws regulating cleanliness.

Overall, it is most especially the poor, the disenfranchised outcasts, and the alienated whom Jesus draws into the embrace of his compassion. He seems to have an insatiable desire for everyone to be able to live freely and wholly. When asked how one can determine the identity of the "neighbor" who, according to the law, is to be "loved as oneself," Jesus tells a story about a wounded traveler who was ignored by the people, whose "religious" duties prevented their tending to his needs. It was an outsider, a Samaritan, who generously cared for the man. Jesus turns the question back on the questioner: which one was neighbor *to* the wounded man? (Lk. 10:29ff.). It is not important to try to define the dimensions of neighborly responsibility, Jesus suggests; what matters is that the eyes of one's heart are open to see a "neighbor" in anyone, with no limits placed on the heart's capacity for compassion. It was a shocking reversal of perspective, which would break down the wall of righteousness that judged some persons outside the limits of God's favor (a Samaritan), and judged observance of religious laws of higher value than responding to a neighbor in need. This is "right relations," according to Jesus. There are no limits to the extent of God's mercy, and equally, there must be no limits to the capacity of the human heart to give expression to that mercy.

Jesus also tells a story about the judgment of the nations in the end times (Mt. 25:31ff.). Presumably, Israel (and we ourselves) are right there in front of the judge, and the judge turns out to be identical with persons in the society who were hungry, thirsty, a stranger, naked, sick, and imprisoned. The judgment of each nation is determined by how they responded

(or failed to respond) to the needy in their midst. Here we see
the deepest principle of covenant morality, but applied now
not just to covenanted Israel, but to all the nations of the
world. Not only are there no limits on God's mercy, but there
are no limits to the necessity that both the individual human
being and the whole of human society be grounded and
steeped in awareness of that mercy.

We have encountered these themes in the Jewish scriptures—in Leviticus, in the prophets. Jesus' life and teaching
bring into clear focus the deepest reality of covenant fidelity in
his own Jewish tradition. He lives "right relations."

Jesus struggled to live and speak the truth no matter what
the cost. Still, over and over he "sternly ordered" everyone—
exorcised demons, people he had cured, his disciples—not to
tell anyone what he had done (cf. Mk. 3:12 passim). Perhaps
he feared that the adulation of the people might weaken him
in his conviction that his mission was completely about God's
power and not his own. Perhaps he felt vulnerable to the lure
of human power.

Matthew's account of the exchange between Jesus and his
disciples at Caesarea Philippi (Mt. 16:13–23) may capture a
moment of discernment in Jesus' life. When Jesus asks his
followers, "Who do people say that the Son of Man is?" and
"but who do *you* say that I am?" he seems to be turning to
them for help in charting his way forward. Maybe he wanted
to check out his own perception of the meaning of his ministry
with those who were closest to him. He asks about the collective perception, and the disciples' response indicated to him
that, at least, the crowd placed him in the category of religious
prophet rather than political messiah. That might be read as a
plus. And in his friends' perception, voiced in Peter's response,
he hears an even deeper insight that suggests to him that it

may be time now to move forward: "You are the Messiah, the Son of the living God."

In today's language, Jesus may have been "asking for feedback." We may imagine that he had been reading the prophet Isaiah, and reflecting on the figure of the "servant" (Is. 42:1–9; 49:1–6; 50:4–11), especially the "suffering servant" image personifying the role of God's covenanted people (52:13–53:12). These passages resonated both with his recollection of God's designating him "my Son, the Beloved" at his baptism and with his increasing sense of his destiny. He had come to face the probability that his own messiahship was to be conformed to that servant image. And after asking his disciples these questions, and sensing in their response some insight and support, he tries to educate them to the next step: he speaks to them of the inevitability of his suffering and death. But Peter is appalled and tries to dissuade him, protesting that he should never allow this to happen.

The vehemence of Jesus' response to Peter may indicate the degree of his vulnerability to that alternative: "Get behind me, Satan [that is, tempter]! You are a stumbling block to me; for you are setting your mind not on divine things but on human things" (Mt. 16:21–23). That note of rare defensiveness on Jesus' part suggests that maybe he had only recently won through to acceptance of the realization that God's future for him involved suffering rejection, and perhaps his owning of that painful path was still fragile. He needed to be able to count on his friends, at least for some minimal sense of understanding and support.

Jesus had to remain alert to the variety of forms taken by "the powers," which had been exemplified in the temptation narrative. This "temptation" by Peter may well have been a critical moment of discrimination for Jesus, when he strug-

gled to stay faithful to his deepest sense of the painful
demands of his call. That struggle with vulnerability is quite
directly engaged in the Garden of Gethsemane, and again and
finally at the time of his actual physical death. His own disciples would desert him. He would need to find his security only
in his own deepest truth, his complete trust in God.

Jesus had rejected people's attempts to identify him as messiah, or to make him king (Jn. 6:15). He had to stay clear: it
was not his own reign that he wanted to preach. At some
point, perhaps the episode depicted above, Jesus accepted the
fact that his own path would inevitably lead in the direction of
suffering and death. He made no attempt to organize a revolution of a political nature, but the bulk of what he was saying
and doing was implicitly if not explicitly revolutionary: it was
undermining the status quo. The responses of the teachers and
leaders became more and more intense and threatening.

Jesus' teaching and his healing were indeed awesome, and
his presence was magnetic, leading people to wonder whether
this man could be the messiah. That in itself was a threat to
those in charge, both Jews and Romans. But more, Jesus
didn't keep the rules of the religious leaders. He challenged
them at every turn, preaching a new order of things in which
God was intimately accessible to anyone who was willing to
forgive and to be forgiven. Jesus wanted to reinterpret the
law to give primacy to human need, and to include in the circle
of God's love those whom the teachers declared unworthy.

But he found the leaders unwilling to listen, rigidly fixed in
their established rules and procedures. He was publicly sub-
verting the authority of their most learned teachers in debate.
In a final act of protest against the profaning of temple worship by those in power who were using it to advance their own
status or make a business of it, Jesus drove out all the people

who were selling and buying in the temple, and overturned the tables of the money changers (Mt. 11:15–18). As a culmination of his brief but provocative street ministry, this ruckus in the temple was the last straw.

And so, of course, the powers-that-be had to get rid of him. He was condemned to crucifixion, the most painful and humiliating death known to the society at the time. It was a clear warning to the public that such subversive behavior was not to be tolerated.

Strikingly the only mention of Jesus as "king" (apart from his refusal of the designation early in John's Gospel) is in the accounts of the trial and crucifixion. An inscription of the title "King of the Jews" is posted on the cross (cf. Jn. 19:19)—the ultimate reversal of worldly power. Jesus' death involved public humiliation as cruel and ignominious as could be imagined. His internal experience of dying seems, according to Mark's (the earliest) account, to have required that he let go of any sense of human security, even of his usually secure knowledge of God's intimate, comforting presence: "My God, my God, why have you forsaken me?" (Mk. 15:34). The moment of his dying asked for the surrender of everything—Jesus' total self-abandonment, his completely naked surrender to the God who had claimed him as "My Beloved."

But, as we know, that was not the end of the story. The God of surprising reversals had not disappeared from history. It was the women who were faithful, having followed him from Galilee, watching from a distance as he died (Mt. 27:55–56). And it was the women who, on the third day, visited his tomb and found it empty, and were the first to proclaim the good news of resurrection (Mt. 28:1–10). Though at first the disciples dismissed their report as women's hysteria, they soon had to deal with the fact: God had raised Jesus from the dead. The powers that had seemed to win on Good Friday were proved ineffective in the last resort. Jesus lives.

Jesus lives, and he was still present with his disciples, though in a new and different mode. After his resurrection, he appeared to them and breathed on them his own Spirit of peace, commissioning them to carry that Spirit into the world just as he had done (Jn. 20:19–23). They experienced his presence especially when they gathered for a meal, reminding them of the number of times he had spoken of the reign of God in the image of a banquet, and reminding them especially of their last meal with him. Then he had identified the bread and wine of the Passover meal with his own body, which, he said, is "given for you," and his blood, "poured out for you," as "the new covenant in my blood" (Mt. 22:19–20). And he had invited them to eat and drink in this same way, to remember him, to live his teaching. They were, in a way mysterious and new, to share his very life.

Little by little, the news spread. The disciples regrouped. "Jesus and his movement maintained the Jewish conviction that with this God new creation can happen at the waiting hands of a small number of very common, even hesitant but emboldened and spirit-filled people."[14] They began the process of remembering what Jesus had said and done, piecing together the meaning of his presence among them. They began to understand that this man was really Emmanuel, God incarnate in Jesus, present in their midst, and that they were to be the witnesses, not just to his past, but to his now-risen presence among them. They formed themselves into a community that tried to practice what Jesus preached: they were to share what they had in such a way that no one among them would be in need (Acts 4:32–37). They were, in other words, to be a communal expression of justice and love, the right relations that God had been steadily promoting throughout Israel's history and which they had seen embodied in the person of Jesus.

God had, then, not given up the centuries-long divine hope that people might live together in peace and justice. The early community was convinced that Jesus' own Spirit remained in and among them, giving them such faith, enthusiasm, and courage that they wanted to share the good news of his teaching, of God's unlimited mercy and forgiveness, of the new life that resulted from his death and rising, of the hope for a transformation of social values. They wanted to share their vision with the whole world! And as they preached in Jerusalem on that Pentecost day, people from all over the world heard the good news, *every one in their own language,* a startling reversal of Babel (Acts 2:5–6). So began the mission of the church, the community of Jesus' followers, to translate "the reign of God" as Jesus had taught and lived it, in communities dedicated to living in the Spirit of Jesus.

This man, Jesus the Christ as he would come to be known, was, for the persons who encountered him, and for those who through them came to know him, the embodiment, the incarnation of Israel's covenanting God—the God cloaked in the ineffable mystery of I AM, the God who brought Israel out of Egypt, the God who was always ready to stand in solidarity with the suffering of humanity and the deep humane impetus for freedom, the God who made a commitment to be present whenever Israel was caring for the poor, the oppressed, the needy, and the alien. This same God is now experienced in the person of Jesus. The Word of God that the prophets had proclaimed now appears in the flesh of Jesus of Nazareth. God's commitment to solidarity with humanity is revealed in a new, deeper, and more decisively intimate mode. "I do not call you servants any longer . . . but I have called you friends," Jesus says, "because I have made known to you everything that I have heard from my Father" (Jn. 15:15). The mutuality of solidarity deepens into friendship, the sharing of personal knowledge, and intimacy, the actual sharing of life. In and through Jesus, solidarity deepens into communion. Presence *with* becomes presence *within*.

Who was this man? According to Albert Nolan,

> [Jesus was] a man of extraordinary independence, immense courage and unparalleled authenticity—a man whose insight defies explanation. . . . No tradition was too sacred to be questioned. No authority was too great to be contradicted. No assumption was too fundamental to be changed. [He was] a man who has the courage of his convictions, a man who is independent of others because of a positive insight which has made every possible kind of dependency superfluous. . . . He did not make authority his truth, he made truth his authority.[15]

But Jesus is not only an external, ethical model for us, one who shows us how to live in God's way. He is that, but much more. The intimate, totally loving presence of God that Jesus knew at the depth of his humanity—that same presence is his promise to everyone who will open their heart to his Spirit, follow in his way, live in communion with him as a branch lives from the vine. In Jesus, God is revealed to be the deepest dimension of our human being. God's presence within will inevitably manifest itself outwardly in a life of caring, of justice, and of mercy.

Jesus embodies what the Hebrew scriptures taught: that love of God and love of one's neighbor are, in the end, inseparable. And both are indispensable. God's love is as accessible and impartial as the sunshine; from God's side, no exception, no barriers. But for Jesus, and for us, the process of a life of openness to this love inevitably requires that one enter consciously and willingly, day by day, into the process of dying, in order to give way to new life for oneself and for others.

Jesus had to face the fact that suffering and death are, in fact, the common destiny of prophets. But more fundamentally, suffering and death are woven into the fabric of all life. His path would require a high degree of commitment and willingness to live in a way that was different, and that would be offensive to conventional standards. His followers would have to let go of a lot of things, attitudes, society's perks, and powers. Following Jesus would mean sharing all that one is and has, giving oneself away, as it were. He taught his followers that if they were going to be faithful, if they really wanted to live to the depths of their own humanity grounded in God — as *he* did — they had better look all that right in the eye. "Those who find their life will lose it," he warned, "and those who lose their life for my sake will find it" (Mt. 10:39), or, in a timeless image, "Unless the grain of wheat falls into the ground and dies, it remains just a single grain" (Jn. 12:24).

Following Jesus means a series of dyings: to one's attachments, to one's fears, to one's self-centered concerns and behaviors. That dying opens onto new life: the continual expansion of our heart's capacity to embrace more and more of creation in our love and the continual deepening of our compassion, our trust and freedom, our grounding in the life of God. The life, death, and resurrection of Jesus teaches all of this. But more, the gift of his Spirit enables us to live in communion of life with Jesus, with one another, and with the rest of creation.

℘ ♋

Let's return to the three lenses suggested in the first chapter, the lenses of science (reason), human solidarity, and communion with the Divine. How does the revelation of God in Jesus relate to each of these lenses? Like the early Christians, we in our time also ask: what are the implications of God's incarnation in Jesus?

First, we can recognize the fundamental Word of love that God speaks to us in Jesus embedded in the whole of creation. There are lessons available to us in the rest of creation: the birds of the air have no part in designing how they are fed, and the lilies of the field receive their beauty as a gift. There is a trustworthy pattern to the creation, each species in its own niche performing its own cooperative function for the good of the whole, all cared for by a Presence that sustains the process in its integrity and goodness.

We can perceive that Word of love in the elemental structure called gravity, which draws things together; we can find it in interacting molecules, hear it in the mating calls of birds, or feel it in the attraction between human beings. Things come together; the coming together changes them; something new results. Everywhere, if we have eyes to see, there is evidence of God's love at work in the whole creation, drawing things together into creative new configurations, little by little seeking ever deeper and more complex unity. Everything on Earth (and, metaphorically at least, even stars and planets, which are born and die) participates in this vast process, continually changing and exchanging, emerging in new form. And so we see that Word of love operating in the principle that *everything in creation exists only by sharing its life.*

Jesus, born of Mary of Nazareth, was made of the same material as we are—his body's fluids the same as those of the oceans, the minerals in his bones the same as Earth's materials, just as ours are. Jesus depended for his breathing on the trees, on the animals and green growing things for his food, on water for his thirst. His life was inseparable from the rest of creation, just as our lives are. God's incarnation in Jesus implies, then, God's presence to the whole of creation whose elemental processes working together kept Jesus alive on Earth and continue to sustain the world as we know it.

As Christians, we affirm that Jesus' divinity is not a compartment separated from his body or from the rest of his life process. God cannot be wholly present in Jesus without being present to the rest of creation. Over centuries, however, and particularly in the West since the Industrial Revolution, we humans began to perceive ourselves as disconnected from the rest of creation, holding ourselves as separate, superior, dominant. We also dualistically separated God from embodiment in the totality of Jesus' being. In doing so, of course, we disconnected Jesus from his own participation in the ongoing process of life's development.

Jesus' life demonstrates precisely, in human behavior, the pattern of life of the whole earth community. What God reveals in Jesus is that when (and insofar as) a human lives in complete and integral alignment with the fundamental principle that everything lives by sharing its life, then God's consistent promise of solidarity with humanity, so central to the Hebrew scriptures, is fulfilled in a completely unexpected way. For his followers throughout the ages, Jesus *is* God-with-us, the embodiment of God. He is the human whose attitudes and actions exemplify not only the solidarity of justice and equality among humans, but also open the way to the possibility of complete communion with the Divine. Such a life embodies justice, love, peace—all that God hopes for humankind; it elicits and brings to fruition the presence and power of the divine within the human/earth community. It manifests "the reign of God."

It is as if God is saying to us: "You humans, if you want to see what a human life looks like when it is lived in complete accordance with my intent, my Word of love which is embedded in creation from the beginning, then *look at Jesus*."

Jesus' whole life was lived according to the principle that life is to be shared, but his mission failed. Or did it? Jesus was crucified because of his fidelity to God's call, and, through his dying, new life entered; the unexpected surprise of resurrection is the completion of the process. Jesus' death and resurrection became the central symbols of the Christian revelation. Christian faith is based in the belief that, just like the rest of creation, the process of human dying yields new life. Our human lives must be aligned with that process.

When we place the death and resurrection of Jesus against that cosmic background of breaking apart/coming together, we see that Jesus reveals to us the human mode of participation in that ongoing process. Like us, he has to struggle with his vulnerability; he has to find his own authentic truth grounded in trust and fidelity to his experience of God's loving presence. He has to keep open to complete willingness to enter into that process in which conscious and willing sharing of one's life is central, and in which not just physical dying, but dying to self is the means to life.

The vulnerability of self-giving is the inescapable pattern and the only way into both solidarity and communion. The pattern, as it expresses itself in humans, requires a willingness to open one's heart to respond to suffering, as the God of Israel always did; it requires engagement in the human struggle for freedom, both internal and personal, and external, in justice and equity in society. Such willingness and engagement call one to action, sometimes costly action, on behalf of the neighbor, near or far. And so the word "neighbor" acquires larger and larger extension: as our hearts open wider, more and more of the human community—and more and more of the whole rest of creation, from the almost invisibly tiny wild-flower to the vast stretches of the cosmos—is drawn into inclusive, encompassing love. The capacity of our hearts can never stop expanding until it is in union with God's own heart, God's infinite love.

The willingness to give of ourselves loosens us up on the inside and yields way, little by little, to a sense of communion. It's as if the letting-go makes an opening, a necessary passage-way that allows new and more expansive life (and love) to enter. The revelation, the example, and most importantly, the redeeming empowerment that Jesus bequeaths to his disciples with the gift of his Spirit is that fidelity to a life of self-giving, even to the point of dying, can be the means to new life for oneself and for the rest of creation. And that is the process— our own daily dying and rising—that opens us to communion of life with God and with the whole creation.

For us, conscious and willing participation in the process of dying and rising is the necessary means of continuing the message and the redemption of Jesus. To commit oneself to that process in one's life is to be a disciple of Jesus.

The church is the community of Jesus' disciples who, through the ages, have committed their lives to living that process of sharing, dying, and rising in the way that Jesus did. In their baptism, Christians are welcomed into a community that is committed to encouraging and enabling in one another an always deeper, more conscious, and more inclusive partici-pation in that dying and rising. Baptism opens the channel to communion: as we descend into the waters of baptism and

emerge, we are sacramentally participating in dying and rising with Christ. And we are making the most fundamental
commitment of our lives: we commit ourselves to willingly
continue that dying and rising process that yields new life.
That fundamental commitment issues in right relations
among people: according to Paul, in baptism there is "no
longer Jew or Greek, there is no longer slave or free, there is
no longer male and female; for all of you are one in Christ
Jesus" (Gal. 3:27). Paul knows as well that the whole creation longs to be included in this liberation (Rom. 8:19–23).
Participation in dying and rising issues in communion.

With every Eucharistic celebration members of the community gather to reaffirm their commitment to participate in
the process that leads to that kind of deep communion. They
use bread and wine, elements that represent the whole of creation: the rain, the sun, the air, the soil, human labor. God's gift
of abundant life is shared with us in and through all of the
many earth processes that finally bring nourishment to our
table. These are the elements used by the Jewish community
at their Passover ritual meals through the ages; they are the
elements Jesus used when he shared his final meal with his
disciples. Jesus proclaimed a new covenant: he identified
these elements with the gift of his own body and his own
blood, his own life, and he invited his disciples to share in that
very life.

As we eat that bread and drink that wine, we are nourished
in the divine self-giving that draws us into union with God,
with the human community, and with the rest of creation. We
commit ourselves to follow in the path of Jesus, and to share
in his life. We say, "Amen. We will be your body, we will continue, in our own lives, to die and rise with and in you. We will
try to help each other to be bread for the world as you were,

sharing our lives with all who are in need." When we celebrate Eucharist, we place ourselves in the service of life; we commit ourselves to live in communion with the whole creation.

The path of Jesus, which we engage in our baptism and reengage in every Eucharistic celebration, is not a path for wimps. Certainly in every age, but blatantly in our age, this is a painfully difficult countercultural stance. Matters of justice and unity and peace are clearly the primary concern of the God we claim to worship in the Judeo-Christian tradition. Do we not have to ask ourselves why and how we have managed to blind and desensitize ourselves to a cultural status quo that promotes militarism, that accepts poverty as a given, that looks unblinking at the looming destruction of Earth's precious life systems? How might we revive our dull and benumbed spirits? How might we enliven them with vision and energy and hope?

We turn now to explore how we as Christians, at this particular time in history, can shape our lives in fidelity to the revelation of God in Jesus. What helps do we need to have in place? What traps can hinder us? What attitudes do we need to cultivate?

Part II

Making the Connections:
Steps on the Path to Global Justice

Chapter Four

The Call to Kinship

All of us Earth creatures on this round planet are, like it or not, "neatly trapped by loving kinship."

The words of Jesus, "Those who find their life will lose it, and those who lose their life for my sake will find it" (Mt. 10:39), resonate in our hearts, along with the words of Micah, "You know what is good; and what does the Lord require of you but to do justice and to love kindness and to walk humbly with your God?" But at times these challenges can seem so large as to boggle our minds, overwhelm our hearts, and paralyze our limbs. What can "right relations" mean in this culture, and against an ever-expanding global horizon? And what does "right relations" mean if, as we have suggested, we are inescapably involved in a universe that is always in process of breaking down and reuniting in new form?

Two things are important to remember as we begin to tackle these questions. The first is that how we see right relations depends upon how we see ourselves. If we see ourselves as autonomous, individual selves on a private journey to God, then right relations will be limited by that definition. The word "neighbor" might then be applied only to those relationships that have immediate impact on our lives: family, friends, close associates. Those close relationships are indeed critical. Real love can never be abstract and generic: it requires concrete, immediate expression in a real-life context. Ordinarily, then, the quality of our relationship to our close neighbors provides the most reliable index of the "rightness" of our relationships.

And yet, if my own existence cannot be separated from the rest of creation, if I am in fact held in being only insofar as I am related to all the rest, and if I think of all the other species not as resources but as "my relatives," then by definition "doing justice" means being in right relation with every living being in my/our journey to God. Now that we are aware of our global responsibility, "my" and "our" are inseparable; the whole community of creation is in fact my neighbor, for our lives are all connected. "Autonomous individual" is only one illusory facet of my identity, which cannot ever be realistically separated from the inclusion of that identity within a larger whole.

Second, the word "process" is very important in this context. A condition of pure justice can never be achieved. We may occasionally win through to a situation of harmony and equilibrium, but that new situation will eventually change too. As we have said, the nature of reality in this creation is such that relations are in continually shifting configurations, changing positions, one thing affecting another, like the scene in a kaleidoscope. These ever-shifting configurations provide the context of our individual participation in the ongoing process of history on planet Earth.

Planet Earth is in a continual process of creation. Focusing on the goal of securing a stable, "peaceful world" in the end only leads to discouragement and disillusionment. It is not that we cannot be inspired by Ezekiel's or Isaiah's visions of a creation permeated by peace and harmony, or by Jesus' vision of "the reign of God." Those visions are given precisely to keep us moving, on track, inspired, and hopeful. They describe the pull of the future, the dream of God that lies like a magnet deep in our innermost heart.

What demands our attention in the present moment, however, is the situation right in front of us. How do we deal with a rebellious child, a bed-ridden spouse, a scrappy neighbor, the impact of church policies that seem intractable, a political process that feels oppressive, or an international scene so fraught with old and new enmities and hostilities that situations seem overwhelming and impossible? Our task is simple, though not at all easy: to discern what is ours to do, and to focus our energies on that concrete situation. All the while, the vision on the horizon, God's dream of shalom, is in fact pulling us forward as a kind of mysterious attractor.

Justice as Kinship

Justice in our legal system is sometimes symbolized in the figure of a blindfolded woman holding scales. But, as Daniel Maguire points out, this image assumes that the scales are empty to begin with, and that the judgments are "impartial" and "objective." They almost never are: judgments are already weighted with the biases of racism, status, gender, and class that are entrenched in our society. Maguire contrasts this placid, impersonal image with the power of the prophet Amos' vigorous directive to "let justice roll down like waters, and righteousness like an everflowing stream" (5:24) — an image of relentless, irrepressible energy. Biblical justice, Maguire says, would "remove the blindfold and see who is tampering with the scales."[16]

In the culture of the United States, justice is probably most often understood as punishment suited to the crime — a life for a life, for instance, as in capital punishment. Moreover, we often assume that law is somehow equivalent to justice, and we fail to make the necessary distinction between legality, morality, and justice. Too often we hear that an action "certainly isn't moral (or just), but it is not illegal." In other words, there is no law on the books that prevents or punishes the action being performed, and there is no recourse other than the long process of trying to make a law to cover the case. While much is honorable and good about our legal system, it has, nevertheless, been shaped by our complex, individualistic society, and it inevitably reflects the inadequacies of our ongoing struggle to sustain a collective sense of the common good.

There is a further limitation. Although the law intends to "do justice," it cannot possibly negotiate all the demands of equity among persons, groups, and corporations in a society as large and complex as ours. In our culture, as in many of the so-called developed countries, the painful reality is that there is little other recourse. People often do not even know their neighbors, and they relate to a diverse and scattered group of acquaintances and contexts. Few local communities are capable of helping people to work out the differences, hostilities, and aggressions that arise.

In recent years, some creative advocates of justice have developed skills of mediation, enabling them to facilitate negotiations between spouses who choose to divorce, for instance, or interpersonal difficulties arising within company staffs that impede their cooperation. Mediators can offer this service alongside, but separate from, the legal system. They can maintain a degree of personal involvement among the parties, with a concern for interpersonal communication and healing. They meet a real need. Still, there are many holes in the fabric of services available to render justice, especially for the poor.

It was no doubt a concern for interpersonal healing that motivated the Truth and Reconciliation Commission in South Africa to bring together victims of apartheid and those most involved, often violently, with keeping that system intact. It was an unusual experiment in applying an interpersonal process to correct a systemic abuse. Sometimes, but not always, these were people who knew each other, whose lives were familiar to and connected with each other. Sometimes, their lives were connected only through the system. In any case, only an interpersonal process could allow opportunity for reconciliation of individuals, and in the long run, this would be the only effective way to change a vicious system. In order to be granted amnesty, the accused had to face the victims or their families; they had to listen to accounts of the impact of their actions. There were tales of unimaginably monstrous cruelty of humans to each other. But there was also overwhelming testimony to the awesome, mysterious capacity of the human spirit for magnanimity, for forgiveness, for transformation.[17]

The situation is similar in some indigenous communities, such as East Timor, where lives or property have been violated. The victims could present their grievances in a community setting. The whole community would hear the case and discuss it, working at it until the elder or the persons in position of responsibility recognized a consensus. They could extend the discussion until there was a sense of closure. To live in harmony with each other was an essential value; the fact that they were a community, and that the convicted person had to return to life in their midst, made all the difference. Much about such a process sounds ideal, and yet even in such close communities there is no possible way to guarantee the healing of memories, or to assure sincere repentance or forgiveness in anyone's heart.[18]

The following incident is recounted by Ella Cara Deloria, describing a process once practiced by the Native American tribe of Dakota (Sioux) Indians. One of the young males in the tribe had been murdered, and the enraged relatives of the slain man gathered to debate how to settle the score. The eldest relative, a man of great influence, sat quietly listening as the tribal members talked themselves out. He reflected back to them what he had heard of their sense of insult and anger and their desire to avenge themselves. They all sat quietly for a while. Then he spoke to them of "a better way":

> That the fire of hate may not burn on in his heart or in ours, we shall take that better way. Go now to your homes. Look over your possessions and bring here the thing you most prize—a horse, say, or weapons, or wearing apparel, or a blanket. Easy ways and empty words may do for others. . . . Let us take the harder way, the better way. . . .
>
> The gifts you bring shall go to the murderer, for a token of our sincerity and our purpose. Though he has hurt us, we shall make him . . . [a relative], in place of the one who is not here. Was the dead your brother? Then this man shall be your brother. Or your uncle? Or your cousin? As for me, the dead was my nephew. Therefore, his slayer shall be my nephew. And from now on he shall be one of us. We shall regard him as though he were our dead kinsman returned to us.

After some time, the slayer was brought to the council tipi, offered the pipe of peace, presented with the gifts, and ritually accepted as a kinsman. The slayer, deeply moved, began to weep. "You see," explains the narrator, "he had been neatly trapped by loving kinship. And you may be sure that he proved himself an even better kinsman than many who had the right of birth, because the price of his redemption had come so high."[19]

This process of peacemaking is characterized by the elder as the "noblest" way, as "harder" and "better," perhaps because it requires the people to call on the deepest resources of their being to internalize and express their identity as one people. This tribe was practicing restorative rather than retributive justice. Talking and listening, venting and being heard, taking time to allow and to process internal change, expressing in an external way the costly acceptance of the offender, and participation in ritual: each of these steps was integral to the process of restoring right relations. They did not then seek vengeance. The right relation was the relationship of kinship, of brother- and sisterhood.

A scene from the Truth and Reconciliation Commission in South Africa offers a modern-day equivalent to this account. An elderly black woman faced several white security police officers, one of whom, Mr. Van de Broek, had just confessed to the brutal murders of both the woman's son and her husband some years before. She had been made to witness her husband's death. His last words had been, "Father, forgive them." A member of the Truth and Reconciliation Commission had turned to her and asked, "What do you want? How should justice be done to this man who has so brutally destroyed your family?" She replied:

> I want three things. I want first to be taken to the place where my husband's body was burned so that I can gather up the dust and give his remains a decent burial.

She paused, then continued:

> My husband and son were my only family. I want, secondly, therefore, for Mr. Van de Broek to become my son. I would like for him to come twice a month to the ghetto and spend a day with me so that I can pour out to him whatever love I still have remaining with me. And finally, I want a third thing. I would like Mr. Van de Broek to know that I offer him my forgiveness because Jesus Christ died to forgive. This was also the wish of my husband. And so, I would kindly ask someone

to come to my side and lead me across the courtroom so that I can take Mr. Van de Broek in my arms, embrace him, and let him know that he is truly forgiven.

As the court assistants came to lead the elderly woman across the room, Mr. Van de Broek, overwhelmed by what he had just heard, fainted. And as he did, those in the court-room—friends, family, neighbors . . . all victims of decades of oppression and injustice—began to sing, softly, but assuredly, "Amazing grace, how sweet the sound that saved a wretch like me."[20]

In both this process and that of the Dakotas, the capacity to forgive and to reclaim the relationship of kinship is the factor that restores and heals. Forgiveness means reclaiming kinship. In fact, recognition of kinship is the deepest truth of justice: the sense of kinship most genuinely constitutes right relations.

In the Gospel of Matthew, Jesus sets a slightly different scene and adds another dimension. Here, the apparent offender is challenged to set things right. "When you are offering your gift at the altar," Jesus says, "if you remember that your brother or sister has something against you, leave your gift at the altar and go; first be reconciled to your brother or sister, and then come and offer your gift" (Mt. 5:23–24). Jesus presupposes a relationship of kinship ("your brother or sister") and connects—as did the prophets of Israel—the harmony of that relationship with the capacity to worship with integrity. Disharmony between persons creates a kind of static, not just between offender and offended but between those persons and God. We cannot separate our relations with our neighbors from our relationship with God: they are a unity, and at some level, perceived or not, disunity creates discomfort.

Just as the "static" of vengeance initially filled the minds and hearts of the offended Dakota tribal members, so Jesus seems to presume that in each of us a kind of internal "static"—strong or muted—arises when we have offended someone. We have broken a bond that will ache until it is repaired. A subtle nagging memory, some feeling of discomfort or disquiet (or maybe guilt, especially in the presence of the offended or offending person) may be the nudging of the Holy Spirit urging one to restore the harmony of right relations, to clear the channels for the message of love.

In our culture of neighborlessness, however, our sensitivity to that static may be impaired or even deadened by the noise and confusion around us, or simply because of the multiple contexts in which our lives are played out. We can easily lose ourselves in other preoccupations and distractions. We may harden our hearts. Sometimes protective psychic processes cover the static because it is too painful to face, as may be the case with abused children or war veterans, who may later be haunted by nightmares. The nudging of the Holy Spirit may go unheeded.

Still, whether it begins with the offended or the offender, reconciliation requires an opening of the heart to reestablish mutuality, inviting a renewal of communication, an unblocking of the channel of love. Real justice is not framed in context of punishment or retribution, but in context of restoration and transformation. As the Catholic bishops asserted in 1971, justice "attains its inner fullness only in love."[21] Right relation is the relation of kinship.

We may grant that, between individuals or in groups or communities where people are known to one another, the process is fairly clear. In these situations, people know their connection with one another, and their moral sense and sense of responsibility to one another are fairly inescapable. People *need* to live in harmonious kinship with each other. We feel the effects if we don't: the whole community of life is endangered.

But when we think of the larger society, and the systems that seem to steer the course of developments nationally and internationally, the responsibility is much more difficult to detect. Trade does bring people and nations together; it does open some pathway of communication and exchange. Nations may be reluctant to go to war with trading partners. In these respects, markets do connect people with each other.

But markets operate on a dollars-and-cents basis. Markets don't worry about what happens to people or to the environment: markets relate to people as consumers, not as kinfolk. Board CEOs generally do not see the effects of their decisions in terms of family breakdown or quality of life; they see their own dividends and salaries. The actual consequences of market connections are, for most of us, unknown, distant, and impersonal. For instance, we may know the external connection between the markets or corporations that provide the clothes we buy and wear, but we have no awareness at all of the distant sweatshops.

More than that, consequences are difficult to foresee. Ordinarily, we develop a moral sense when we *see*, when we experience the effects of our actions. But who can see an immediate effect of driving a car to the supermarket? Which car's exhaust can be blamed for global warming? Which one of us is responsible for the sweatshops in Indonesia? How do we do justice in a world of global responsibility? The scale of our collective moral responsibility has increased enormously in the last century, and it continues to expand. We have not yet fully awakened to the kind of shift that this new world scene requires of us. The experience and the questions it raises are still too new.

Our world has become both smaller and larger. It is smaller because we are now aware that we are, after all, just one minuscule planet, all of us together. But it is larger because we realize, precisely, that we are all one family of life on Earth, and everything we do has upon all the rest an impact that we cannot possibly track.

That widening of awareness requires a reframing of our sense of justice. Not only do we now have information about wars, poverty, and injustice that exist all over the world, but we are, to a greater or lesser extent, implicated in them. We have to become aware of the larger forces shaping our reality: the systems, the corporations, the entrenched biases of racism, classism, and sexism. How can we respond in right relation to them? How can we work to bring them into right relation?

And as we begin to recover our awareness of relationship to all the species that form our life-support system, we also have to ask questions about eco-justice. How do we do justice in the context of the whole creation? How do we learn to respect all other species and enable them to make their particular contribution to the whole community of life?

In order to live justly, in right relation with the whole creation, we have to develop new sensitivities. We have to learn—as a species—how to practice cooperation rather than domination; we have to learn how to respect the rights of other species that we may have heretofore simply dismissed. In short, we have to learn to live together, human and other species. There is a huge, very urgent task ahead of us. We are, only very slowly, beginning to understand and to feel the impact of the issues that face us, to sense how much and how profoundly our minds and hearts need to change. We are only beginning to know what questions to ask and how to ask them.

We are still at some distance from being able to answer those questions. We need the deepest wisdom available to the human species in order to be able to address the crisis of our time. That is why it is so important for us to probe deeply the spiritual resources available to us in our religious tradition, to work together toward the sense of communion—the "loving kinship"—that alone can provide the attitudes and energies to create conditions of justice, peace, and unity in the world.

The truth is that all of us Earth creatures on this round planet are, like it or not, "neatly trapped by loving kinship." The condition of the planet makes it evident that "to care" is a responsibility entrusted to our species, not as an option for an elite group, or for one religiously motivated group, but for all of us humans. It will be useful for us to hold up for ourselves the value and even the necessity of "the better way," so that our understanding of justice is formed by our appreciation of our kinship with all creation, and grounded in the sense of responsibility we all have for one another.

Chapter Five

Monitoring Inner Motivations

*You can't stand in the midst of the world and struggle for fun-
damental change unless at the same time, you are standing
in your own space and looking for change within.*

Howard Thurman

We can begin, then, to look at our collective responsibility in this present moment. The question we can
ask ourselves is: how do you, and how do I, participate in the
universal process (described earlier) of breaking down and
building up, which is going on in the whole creation?
Conscious participation in this process is our human way to
achieve right relations. As members of the Body of Christ,
our alignment with that ongoing exchange gives shape and
content in our time to the dying and rising of Jesus, the continuing redemption of creation.

The frenetic character of our society keeps many if not
most people working more than one job, rushing from place
to place, moving from distraction to distraction. Something in
the forced pace is subtly demonic. It keeps our minds and our
senses under siege to the constant bombardment of noisy
advertising, superficially created desires, wants, needs, eating, buying, consuming. And when we are frenetic, we are
unable to get our bearings, to reflect on why (or how) we are
doing what we do. We don't have time to remember that we
live on a finite planet, and to be grateful to and for the many
fragile life forms that graciously contribute their lives for our

sustenance. We don't have time to see beneath surfaces or to listen to our hearts.

We cannot underestimate the difficulty involved in trying to live a commitment to an alternative lifestyle. Simply to become conscious of the feeling of breathlessness and powerlessness, to be aware of the clash of priorities and of the lures to accumulate more than we need—that in itself requires steady effort. To be in conversation with like-minded friends is an absolute necessity.

A first step, then, is to gather or join a group or community of persons who have a desire to translate the gospel's values of social justice into their lives. In some ways, this may be the largest hurdle, given the rampant individualism and the relative lack of community in the culture. Moreover, there is no "how-to" formula for success. The intention is to gather with some regularity to ponder the application of the Scripture to daily life, to share information about local and global issues of social justice, to pray together, to share both personal and social concerns, to encourage collaboration in social action, and to keep perspective and humor and hope alive when the going gets hard. In short, the intention is to empower each other to live the gospel. A commitment to faithful participation is the hoped-for goal.

There may be different kinds of groups, and different levels of sharing and trusting. Some are just "groups," and some become genuine communities, with a host of variation. There are decided advantages to a parish-based group, especially the advantage of potential impact upon the rest of the congregation. But the group might also take the form of a neighborhood ecumenical group, a circle of friends, perhaps even friends of different faith persuasions. There may be temporary groups whose sole purpose is to deal with a specific problem, such as racial resentments in a neighborhood. Such a group might well find its initial purpose expanding to include spin-off areas, and their identity might evolve as their relationships deepen and become more committed. Years of meeting, talking, sharing, praying, and acting together are often required in order to develop the quality of trust that can deepen into a solid sense of spiritual unity. In any case, if a group is to remain together, members will almost inevitably be drawn into deeper levels of sharing and trusting, and a deeper sense of kindred S/spirit will develop among them.

Groups or communities typically have moments of difficulty and perhaps discomfort, as well as moments of gracious unity that enable them to test the level of their commitment to stay together and to work it out. For a variety of reasons—families moving, the inability to establish effective group dynamics, or real ideological or personality conflicts—such groups will change over the years. Sometimes they dissolve. The point is not so much that we have to have a group of a certain kind or duration, but simply that we need steady friends, connections to help us find our voices, to share our failures and successes, to keep our inner compass pointed in the direction of gospel values, and to keep alive our dreams and hopes. We need others to help us discern where to put our energies, find what might be effective ways to protest, and together invent creative alternative lifestyle initiatives.

In order to maintain perspective, such a community would have to cultivate the kind of discernment that keeps one eye on the big picture of political systems, whether in the church, the nation, or the world of international corporations. Questions of "how does this affect the poor?" "who stands to gain?" "who is making money in this arrangement?" "where is the power located?" "who will gain from keeping things this way?" or "who would lose if it changes?" are the lenses through which current systems must be evaluated.

Frequently a commitment to social justice grows out of a concrete experience of the suffering caused by injustice, either to oneself or to others. When we can identify with the feeling of powerlessness, frustration, and rage felt, for example, by a single mother unable to earn a salary equal to the cost of day-care (let alone rent and food), or by a homeless family unable to find housing they can afford, we begin to question the systems that keep people trapped in those situations. We begin to question political processes, legislation, politicians, corporations. We begin to imagine alternatives for change. Firsthand experience for members of the group keeps discussions and resolutions from becoming abstract and speculative; contact with the people who are actually adversely affected by present policies—persons who are unemployed and "unemployable," the poor, the homeless, abused women and children, persons marginalized because of race, gender, or sexual orientation— such personal contact leads us to begin to make connections and to form a social conscience. So the journey begins.

A group needs to look for the connections between things: Is there a connection between the incidence of childhood cancer, polluted water, and the large paper-producing company upstream? Is there a connection between rich absentee landlords, the condition of housing in slums, and street crime? Is there a connection between a U.S. company's privatization of water in Bolivia and increasing poverty and hunger among the Bolivian people? Is there a connection between the millions made in a year by the CEO and his company's union-busting strategies? Obviously, the answer is quite likely yes. The point is that to deplore the situation or to treat the childhood cancer is not enough. One has to look into, through, and beyond the situation to its causes in order to imagine alternatives and to chart the steps toward change.

Sometimes a chain of connections needs to be explored. At all levels—from the individual who is hurt, up the line to the corporate board or the political machinery—the need for exposure and change becomes apparent.[22] In any case, understanding the system and how it works is a critical part of the work to be done. And that is work better done by many heads and many hands than by one.

Along with individual contact and alertness as to how systems cause injustices, there is a third area of important awareness: the role of the media in shaping our cultural perceptions and values. Practically speaking, that process of making connections requires information, and reliable information can be difficult to obtain; media sources are favorite vehicles of propaganda. "To control a nation, you don't have to control its laws or its military. All you have to do is control who tells the nation its stories. Television tells most of the nation most of its stories most of the time," says George Gerbner.[23] It is important to be aware of what is currently offered in the news by mainstream media, because that is what is shaping public opinion and collective values. However, it is equally important both to support and to have access to alternative radio, TV channels, news magazines, Web sites, and books that take the risks of exposing dishonesty and injustice and that promote public awareness of the necessity for values of cooperation, nonviolence, respect for diversity, recognition of human rights, and ecological sensitivity. To be tuned in to both mainstream and popular media as well as alternative sources allows one to appreciate the complexity of the questions, and to avoid shallow or facile attempts at solutions.

These three areas—the awareness acquired by experiential

contact, the understanding of the influence of systems, and alertness to media impact—need to be developed. Then they need to be brought together with study and reflection on the scriptures and the social teaching of the church. All of this background allows for the development of a social conscience that is prepared to critique the status quo, ready to "speak the truth in love," as Paul put it, to challenge the power structures that hold unjust systems in place. A group that is consciously working to exchange information, learning together, and keeping each other honest is the best possible context of preparation for action for justice.

Stated in this fashion, the agenda sounds overwhelming. But we are assuming that the process of formation takes a lifetime, and that this ongoing learning becomes part and parcel of a Christian commitment, becoming more finely tuned, and growing wider and deeper with the years.

Obviously, no one person can cover all those bases and have time left for eating and sleeping and a little sharing with the family. That is why groups are so important: people have to share perceptions, share information, work together to arrive at common understandings, and try to discover appropriate attitudes, postures, and strategies where response is possible and necessary. To repeat: this is hard work, and it requires steadiness, firm purpose, and a shared sense of priority commitment.

No one can do it alone, and equally, no community can do it to perfection. At their very best, our efforts will always be limited. We need to remember, then, that we aren't the only dancers on the stage and that our "troupe" is just one very minuscule part of a kaleidoscopic whole. We need the firm conviction that each of us is playing a role that is essential to the working out of the whole.

The Personal Dynamics of a Spirituality of Justice

At this point we want to begin to focus on some of the inner dynamics of developing a faith life in which action for justice plays an integral role. Here it is critical to recognize the interplay between our engagement in the outer world and our own inner psychological/spiritual processes. While anyone concerned about justice needs to confront the reality of systems and their power, we cannot afford to make the mistake of locating all the problems of the world outside ourselves. Although systemic evil acquires a power of its own,[24] every systemic evil has its roots in the hearts of each participating individual. Here we focus on the individual practitioner, or rather, the individual-in-community, trying to hold in tension the relationship between the outer and the inner, society and person.

If keeping one eye on the power structures and systems of the outer world is important, it is equally important for the members of the group to keep the other eye on their own relationships and investments—financial, ideological, and personal. After all, most of the people reading this book enjoy the some of the fruits of those systems: the advantages of available and cheaply priced clothes that may be the product of sweatshop labor, a wide variety of foods that may be grown by peasants who live in poverty, and gasoline that may come from exploited oilfields abroad. Some readers may also profit from stock market dividends that result from investment in a tangled web of unjust corporation ventures.

How do we develop the capacity not just to see the reality of injustice in the outer world, but to recognize as well the multiple levels of collusion and cooptation that affect our own lives? How are *we* hooked into the system? What are we (what am I) gaining and enjoying as perks from the system? How do I have to change? What do I stand to lose? Where does an issue touch me and my family personally, make me squirm, elicit a feeling—sometimes even subliminal and not fully conscious—of reluctance or fear? It is sometimes easy to engage in heady ideological or ethical critique of large, objective systems, and not to notice—or, in fact, completely ignore—the small, nettling unease just below the surface that would serve as a warning that there's dangerous muddy water ahead. It is not always easy to detect in our own attitudes and behaviors the evidence of the systems' power over *us*. In such cases, justice-minded persons will need to have developed the capacity for attending to their own "stuff." How do we do this work?

Jesus was, apparently, aware of these difficulties:

> Do not judge, so that you may not be judged. . . . Why do you see the speck in your neighbor's eye, but do not notice the log in your own eye? Or how can you say to your neighbor, "Let me take the speck out of your eye," while the log is in your own eye? You hypocrite, first take the log out of your own eye, and then you will see clearly to take the speck out of your neighbor's eye.
>
> (Mt. 7:1–5)

Jesus' warning applies with equal strength to our readiness to condemn the systems that operate in the larger world, as well as the flaws and failures of the near neighbor.

Can we identify other countries as evil if we do not recognize the oppressive policies perpetrated by our own country, both here and abroad? Can we blame oppressive governments if we do not attend to our own oppressive behaviors at home, at work, here in the group that wants to work for justice? Can we rail against corporate greed if we are not equally sensitive to the evidences of greed in our own hearts and lives? Can we attack the warmongering of nations if we are not alert to the violence—whether overt or masked in sarcasm or dismissive responses—that characterizes some of our own interactions? Projecting our stuff onto persons or systems in the outer world is the easiest and the most deceptive way of keeping ourselves feeling good about ourselves . . . and superior to others.

Every single evil we can identify in the outer world is present also, at least in the form of tendency or capacity, if not in our behavior, then in ourselves. Groups dedicated to peacemaking are torn apart by their own power struggles and differences of opinion. Persons dedicated to working with group conflict resolution processes see their own marriages fall apart. We simply cannot afford to relax vigilance on either the outer front or the inner one. Holding together the macro and the micro, the social and the personal, the mission-oriented and the therapeutic, the outer and the inner: these balancing acts must remain in the foreground consciousness of any person and any group that intends to work for justice. Justice is, after all, about right relations. It applies with equal strength to every area of our lives.

Let's pause and consider anger, an emotion that is a frequent visitor to persons willing to engage in issues of social justice. When we open our minds and hearts to the damage done to ourselves, other humans, or to the integrity of the whole creation by unjust, greed-driven behaviors and systems, we are quite likely to experience anger as a first response. Contact with the suffering of others can evoke in us feelings of powerlessness, frustration, and rage born of empathy with their situation. Why? Because we are in fact connected. Our sense of kinship is being awakened. The arising of those feelings signals that somehow life—our life—is being threatened or violated. If we were not open to the connection, we would feel no response. The anger, therefore, is arising spontaneously out of a felt sense of unity that we simply have not recognized.

Although our culture tends to regard frustration and anger as negative emotions, their presence in us in response to injustice is perfectly natural and appropriate. The prophets of Israel and Jesus himself responded with anger. Jeremiah internalized God's word as "an incurable wound"; he was filled with indignation (Jer. 15:18, 17). Jesus, in a face-off over his willingness to cure on the sabbath, "looked around at them with anger; he was grieved at their hardness of heart" (Mk. 3:5). According to Daniel Maguire, if we do *not* feel anger, "The prophets would say we have a problem with heartlessness. . . . When we are not angry in the face of injustice, we love justice too little."[25] But Jesus' attitude was not to destroy the bad guys. His response was never to stop loving, never to stop trying to heal, always speaking the truth of what he knew.

Anger is a natural response to threat or fear. Fuming, stewing, ranting, and raving may provide some outlet, but anger is energy for life that begs to be converted into action. The action could be vengeance and violence, which look to past injustice. Or it could be action that aims to remedy and restore, which looks to the future. The role of healthy anger is ordinarily a temporary one. It is a warning signal that something is wrong, and it is intended to spur us to corrective action. If it endures, however, if it burrows into our system and festers, we little by little become hardhearted and rigid. Eventually a cold and stony hatred may develop in us, drying up the wellspring of love. We could begin to take on the characteristics we perceive in those we name oppressors.

But if we heed our anger as a signal, we are often spurred

to action that deepens in us the capacity for compassion. We thus act out of the truth of our being: that we are united as kin to all creation.

We probably always need to keep an eye out for the appearance of feelings of resentment and anger. Often we project our anger at systems onto administrators or leaders, whether they are in government, church, or our business offices. We allow them to become in our imaginations bigger-than-life, totally evil figures. In reality, they too are only struggling human beings, but we want to distance them from ourselves. We find it difficult to acknowledge *our* unity with *their* kind of humanity.

The old adage, "Love the sinner, hate the sin," is a wise one, but more difficult than it sounds. We have to try to open our hearts to "walk in their moccasins," their temperaments, influences, life histories—even though we find it a very uncomfortable exercise. In other words, while not condoning their injustice, we have to open ourselves to compassion for them as fellow, fallible human beings.

Holding our anger before God in our prayer *and* asking for the gift of compassion are often the best we can do. Suffering frustration because of our inability to change ourselves can be a great source of humility, leading us to feel compassion for ourselves, even as we pray to feel compassion for others.

Work for justice requires that we make judgments, that we name the evil we see and call it evil, whether it exists in the outer world or in a neighbor's patently discriminatory behavior. But caution is necessary! The danger of making those moral judgments is that they often arise from a posture of separateness, "we good guys" judging "them," the bad guys. Such judgment seems almost inevitably to give us a sense of superiority, a kind of power that easily morphs into arrogance:

"We're doing it right, and they're doing it wrong" equals "We're better than they are" or "I'm better than you are."

Let's transpose Jesus' parable about the Pharisee and the tax collector (Lk. 18:9–14) into a modern scenario. Maybe Jesus would tell the story this way:

Two men were praying in the church. One man, up in the front pew, was a respected senior bank official, who participated in parish novenas, served on the parish council, and regularly and generously contributed time, talent, and treasure to the parish. He and his family always came to Mass together every Sunday and nearly filled the pew. The other, kneeling in the back, was manager of a firm that collected rent from people in low-income housing complexes, whose work involved threatening, dunning, and garnisheeing wages from the poor.

The first man felt very complacent, and when he prayed, he expressed to God his gratitude that he was able to do things right. He kept the rules, tried to do everything that was expected. He knew he was held up as an exemplary Catholic for the rest of the parishioners. He felt a kind of pity, verging on scorn, for the fellow in the back who, he knew, was involved in all kinds of shady deals. The fellow in the back, however, was feeling sad and shamed. He was aware of the conflict between his love for his family and the need to feed them, and the behaviors his job required him to act out. All he could think to do was ask for God's mercy. And Jesus concludes his story: "I tell you, this man went down to his home justified rather than the other; for all who exalt themselves will be humbled, but all who humble themselves will be exalted."

The parable is a classic tale of judging, on several levels. The first man finds some pleasure in comparing himself with the other and clearly judges himself superior. The second man judges only himself. The story tells us that the first man's sense of superiority came from doing things right, keeping the rules. What made the first man "grateful" was his own doing, his own self-congratulatory goodness; he's looking at himself in the mirror and patting himself on the back. The second man can't tout any good deeds; he can't rely on the merits of his action to earn God's favor. He can only acknowledge his need of God's mercy. But, Jesus says, asking for—and receiving—God's mercy is all that is needed.

For us who read this parable, there is a strange twist: if we recognize in ourselves that tendency to self-righteousness, we are already on track to become the sinner begging for God's mercy, whom Jesus declares "justified." On the other hand, if we try to assume the role of the second man in the interest of "getting it right," but then quietly feel complacent about our own humility, we have already popped back into the role of the first man. The story leaves us in a quandary. We can't get God on our side no matter how hard we try.

Maybe the story is saying that it is not for us to rate ourselves on some curve of moral accomplishment, nor to compare ourselves with anyone else's moral standing. As soon as we do that, we begin to imagine God as a cosmic scorekeeper, and we ourselves as the source of our own virtue. We begin to think our security lies in certain kinds of behavior that are calculated to win God's favor. We watch ourselves doing good. We get in our own way. Maybe that's the definition of a do-gooder.

It is not that our actions do not matter. They matter very much. But action is not the only thing that matters: where the action comes from within us, the kind of energy that is communicated through the action also makes a great deal of difference. Love is, always, a gift, a grace evoked from some mysterious place in ourselves, by some mysterious process we do not control. We can never make love happen. When we are most acting out of love, we are least conscious of ourselves. When we self-consciously pride ourselves on the good that we do, or on "doing it right," that "self" gets in the way of love. Love, at its best, is unself-conscious.

When our actions, even very commendable actions on behalf of justice, come from a place of self-conscious goodness or superiority, they put us in the position of the first man, who, Jesus suggests, did not find favor before God. But in actual fact, most of our good actions have at least some degree of self-conscious praise mixed in. What can we do?

We have to develop an inner monitor, a "watching place" within, a kind of internal radar screen that reflects for us the rise and fall of ego investments. It records for us the subtle movements of thought and feeling that separate us from each other and from our own deepest and truest self. For instance, you may feel a little inner tweak if you exaggerate your own role as a hero in some event, or if you say something that isn't true or is unnecessarily unkind about someone else in order to make yourself feel more important. Some quiet (or loud) inner voice might say, "Hmm . . . that wasn't true, was it? Why did I say that?" Or, when the vehemence or passion of your response seems out of proportion, the "watching place" might say "Hmm . . . why am I so emphatic and opinionated here? Is there something hiding beneath the surface of my conscious motivation? Why do I feel so defensive?" Sometimes we call it conscience. Whatever we call it, inner watching of this sort keeps us alert to detect the very subtle tendency of the ego to latch onto "good behavior" as a source of security.

That monitor keeps an eye on motivation, watching the ego come onto the screen and then disappear again, we hope, noting the rise of self-consciousness and self-investment. It will signal when desire to prove ourselves takes on an edge of competition, or when a subtle feeling of "better than" or "inferior to" insinuates itself into our holiest motivations. Such feelings separate us from others and indicate that we are comparing, grading ourselves.

Usually we only need to note the feelings and let them go; occasionally, we may want to reflect back on them in a time of journaling or prayer to identify the fear or insecurity that might have triggered them. But it is important not to fixate on them: becoming preoccupied with our feelings only increases our focus on ourselves.

Again, this monitoring is a very quick inward motion, simply noting; it does not take a lot of time, and it need not distract us from engagement in discussion or action. It is a kind of backdrop awareness to whatever is going on outside ourselves.

Sometimes, however, if a group is engaged in serious discerning or is experiencing a lot of anger, or struggling with some difficulty, it may be helpful to call for a moment of quiet so that people can get in touch with what is going on inside themselves. A little time of quiet allows the opportunity to distinguish what is, in fact, simply my opinion from the truth or, more likely, to distinguish *my* truth from *the* truth. This is a very critical kind of discernment, for we are most apt to confuse them. A moment of quiet enables us to recover a sense of perspective and to diminish some of the intensity that builds up when we begin to confuse our own way with God's way. If everyone has a chance to check their own investments and rein them in, it may create space for the wisdom of the Holy Spirit to enter.

This interaction between what goes on in the outer world in our conversations and involvements and our internal responses and reactions is the privileged site of our spiritual growth. As we encounter the world, we have the opportunity to recognize our tendencies and motivations, both the generous and the self-centered ones. We can learn to identify our self-serving mechanisms, even very subtle ones, which siphon off the genuine energy of love. We begin to appreciate our own need for liberation from the bondage of our compulsions and our self-deception, and we can place ourselves just as we are before God, opening ourselves to the mercy that is always working to free us, to deepen our capacity for love.

At ever deeper levels, we become aware of ego investments that attach to the goals we set for actions. We plan, we strategize, we act because we want something to change. We know our cause is good. We want our energies to have some effect; we want to make a difference. That is, surely, not unreasonable. But almost inevitably, if we look carefully, we find that a good part of our interest and willingness to engage in an action is attached either to some (perhaps subtle) self-interest, or at least to having things come out the way we think they should. Both of these are attachments that can corrode our good intentions.

When we have some self-interest (even unconscious) staked in a project, we very likely wish to force our will on a situation, to make something happen according to our wishes or our plan. That is simply another form of self-righteousness, equating our own agenda with God's, thinking that our plan is God's plan, and that it needs to be as I will it to be.

But what if the project fails to accomplish any visible result? What if no one even notices? What if it ends in a fiasco? If the action doesn't turn out the way we planned, we may be discouraged and lose hope. If it doesn't attract sufficient attention or doesn't get the right publicity, we might find ourselves feeling strangely disappointed. If we don't feel enough support from our church or our collaborators, we may feel angry, abandoned, or disillusioned. Or, if we judge it "successful," we may experience a high . . . followed by a sense of depression as the heroics wear off.

None of this should surprise us. Try as we might, some little corner within us wants to be God, wants the world to behave according to our designs and wishes. We always have some desire to be recognized as good or effective, maybe even heroic. Even if we can't find in ourselves any trace of self-investment, we congratulate ourselves for being so pure. The ego game is one we cannot win.

Nor do we have to. Mercifully, we don't have to wait until our hearts are perfectly clear and pure before we engage in action. If that were so, we would never move an inch. All that is required is that we do our best, trying to be faithful and honest. And we do need to keep always in view the dynamic and reciprocal relationship between action and reflection/prayer, paying attention to what goes on within us in the process of our active engagements: together they provide the learning context and content that clarify and deepen us as instruments of God's love and justice.

It doesn't matter whether we speak of highly visible actions of civil disobedience that risk imprisonment, or simply actions of quiet generosity or courage that are more or less costly personally but have no visibility whatever. Any such action in the following of Jesus can reveal to us the contours of the inner landscape in which we journey. The way is always more a process of letting go than of achieving or accumulating. It may well involve more losing than finding: Jesus spoke of it that way, warning us that losing ourselves is the key to finding ourselves. Our action for justice provides the opportunity to go a step deeper into the dying-to-self and rising to new life that is our baptismal commitment.

The ability to be in touch with our feelings and motivations requires steady practice. It is a highly individual process. Some people want to have quiet time and space, perhaps a journal, to reflect on what they experience. Others want "processing time" with a trusted friend or friends. Many people appreciate both private time and sharing time. Regular meeting with a good spiritual companion or director can be an immense help in determining what form of prayer and meditation is suitable for a particular person at a particular time, and keeps us honest about our fidelity to practice.

Prayer time, when we let the Scripture probe us, is bedrock discipline:

> The word of God is living and active, sharper than any two-edged sword, piercing until it divides soul from spirit, joints from marrow; it is able to judge the thoughts and intentions of the heart.
>
> (Heb. 4:12)

We need to place ourselves regularly, with all of our goodness and our garbage, just as we are in the presence of the Mercy. For God knows and loves us just as we are: knows us through and through. As the psalmist wrote, "You formed my inmost parts," and "knit me together in my mother's womb" (Ps. 139). However one works at it, an inner "watching place" is an essential tool in the cultivation of courageous honesty and integrity, and in cutting through the layers of self-protecting mechanisms that bedevil our best efforts to love.

Chapter Six

The Path to Compassion

When God had finally completed the creation of the world and had washed the mud off his hands, he sat down beneath one of the trees in Paradise and closed his eyes. "I am tired," He murmured; "why shouldn't I rest for a minute or two?" He commanded sleep to visit him; but at that instant a goldfinch with red claws came, perched above Him, and began to cry. "There is no rest, no peace; do not sleep! I shall sit above Thee night and day, crying, There is no rest, no peace; do not sleep! I will not allow Thee to sleep, for I am the human heart."[26]

What do I really want? That question often lies buried deep in our hearts, underlying much of our restless craving and consuming. Layers and layers of "desires" are at work within us. Some are obvious: they are the things our society seduces us to buy and accumulate, and the self-images that we have internalized, often unconsciously. Each of us can make our own list of those: clothes, gadgets, cars we think we need to have, or how we need to look, smell, and act so as to be desirable or (more modestly) merely acceptable in the culture. But there are other, more subtle internal layers: the need for attention, to be first, important, recognized, "special," to stand out, to be needed. Those are just some of the infinite variations our egos serve up. Equally, however, the perception of oneself as weak, inadequate, worthless, or unworthy works in exactly the same way. These self-perceptions, both lofty and lowly, keep us focused on ourselves, albeit only at opposite

91

ends of the spectrum. They are facets of the same thing: focus
on the self and its insatiable desires. They are all connected
with our sense of security, trying to find it by having and getting, and that is where work needs to be done.

In prayer and reflection, we continually return to the question: What is our deepest desire? What is the real desire of our
hearts? The deepest desire of the human heart is, really,
always for God. Through a myriad of distorted lenses, on a
series of often tortuous, crooked paths, our stubbornly restless
hearts are always trying to find the way to God.

What do we want? Hidden under and within our varied
cravings is a persistent need, a restlessness to be in right relation with the rest of creation. The truth of our lives is that we
are so completely bound up with one another that we cannot
move or act or think without affecting each other. God's commitment to be in solidarity with the creation means that God
is intimately involved, from within, in the intertwined jour-
neys of our lives. Our need for God cannot be separated from
our longing to be connected, in relationships of love and harmony, with each other and with the whole creation. That is the
way God is (continually) creating us.

Until we are living in right relationship, we are restless,
striving, fighting for our lives. God—the God of Israel's
covenant, the God incarnate in Jesus Christ—is restless
within us, as long as we are out of sync. Inevitably, then, our
life work has to be a process of seeking to align ourselves in
right relations with the rest of creation. Relationships are not
right if they do not recognize the integrity, the unique pre-
ciousness, of each other being. What obscures that recognition
is our tendency to ignore the relatedness and to cling to our
own turf, both inner and outer, seeking to find security. We
fear that unless we shore up our self-sufficiency and inde-

pendence, unless we strive and compete, unless we focus on getting things for ourselves, we will not survive.

As we have seen, we always need to connect the outer arena of social action with parallel inner work. Remember that the synoptic Gospels presented the confrontation of Jesus with Satan at the beginning of his ministry. He was tempted, in three episodes, to use his power as Son of God in self-serving ways. We suggested that these temptations may not have been isolated instances preparing him for his ministry, but rather that they represent in cameo fashion the continual discernment of motivation that was required of Jesus. If he was to be faithful to his vocation to announce the reign of God, he would have to be careful to stay grounded in communion with God, and clear of motivations that were simply self-protective or self-serving. Steady discernment and renunciation in his use of power would be essential.

The case is no different for us. We must deal honestly with our own motivations. If we are to recognize the subtle traps of ego stuff; if we are not to get caught in righteous and messianic pretensions of saving the world; or, conversely, if we are not to be paralyzed by fears of our own inadequacies, we have to take our inner life as seriously as we do our actions in the world. New aspects of our own self-interested motivations are continually revealed. Simply recognizing the mixture of motivations, simply acknowledging them humbly before God and/or before one another serves to loosen their hold. We can let them go, at least for the moment.

Paradoxically, our security does not lie in grasping, but in letting go. Our security lies in the awareness that everything, at every moment, is God's gift. Our life is not our own; we cannot claim it, but only receive it as it is given, at every moment. We do not belong to ourselves, but, in God, to the whole of creation in a relationship of deep mutuality and reciprocity. Our life grows and deepens only as it is shared, consciously and willingly, freely and generously. And so to loosen our clutch on life, to relax comfortably and gratefully into the awareness that we are being held in an immense web of relationships, that is where our security lies.

As we have seen, it is ordinarily through our relationships with others that we are confronted with the subtle ways we try to secure ourselves. When we find ourselves trying to take on the responsibility for changing the world, or even for controlling a situation or another person, we have the opportunity to recognize our own insecurity in operation. Each time we find ourselves wanting recognition, wanting to play a leading role or to be a hero, we identify and let go of a move to secure ourselves. Each time fear keeps us silent when we know we should speak, we know we're seeking false security. Equally, each time we demean our own capacities and refuse to risk involvement, we are seeking security through self-protection. As we become aware of these inner dynamics, we encounter ourselves. The process of continuing self-revelation exposes us to ourselves little by little. We have the opportunity to clear the channel of some of the dross that clogs our life's energy and to allow love to move freely through, unimpeded by our self-centered preoccupations. We can relax. We can trust.

Purifying motivations is inner work of the highest order, and it inevitably keeps one in a posture of humility before God. To be able to act simply because it is given to one to do — not without a goal, certainly, but without attachment to a goal — requires deep, mature faith. It is faith placed not in our own resources, nor in the action itself, but in the power of truth and the power of love that works through us . . . not *with-*

out us, to be sure, but through us, when we trust. To learn to
act from that posture of faith is the work of a lifetime, the
result of thoughtful action in tandem with prayer and honest
discernment and reflection.

Thomas Merton's advice to Jim Forest is meditation material for every activist. Writing to Forest about his activities in
the peace movement in 1966, Merton suggested that Forest
needed to "get free from the domination of causes and just
serve Christ's truth," adding that then he would not be
"crushed by *inevitable disappointments*" (emphasis mine). And
further, Merton writes:

> All the good you do will come not from you but from the fact
> that you have allowed yourself, in the obedience of faith, to be
> used by God's love. Think of this more and gradually you will
> be free from the need to prove yourself, and you can be more
> open to the power that will work through you without your
> knowing it.[27]

A "power that will work through you without your knowing it." That is the kind of power that Jesus exercised: the
power of a life that is faithful to truth. This is the power of a
love that remains trustingly grounded in God no matter what
the cost, a love that is stronger than death, and that yields —
whether or not we see or experience it — Life in abundance for
the rest of creation. It is our faith that such a power is possible for us. But the condition of such power is our participation
in the dying, the self-emptying of the Body of Christ, through
which the real power of God's total and compassionate love
can reach the world. What we cling to as our personal power
must be placed at the service of the power of God.

Constant vigilance is essential. How often did Jesus
admonish his followers, "Stay awake!" We need to keep both

eyes open. Still, vigilance doesn't imply a rigid, tense, effort-laden attitude. Our striving to be good—though indeed, we must try—will never of itself "work." Never making a mistake, always being clean and pure, achieving perfection: these are not the goal. What a relief it is to hold together Matthew's rendition of Jesus' teaching, "Be perfect as your heavenly Father is perfect" (5:48), with Luke's version of the same: "Be merciful, just as your Father is merciful" (6:36). The only "perfection" God wants for us is the perfection of a love that we can never claim and can never attain by our own efforts, but can only receive. Love is always grace.

Difficulties and failures remind us of the limitations of our own good intentions, our impotence to save ourselves. Such awareness often forces us to recognize our own perpetual need for healing, and to turn to one another and to the all-encompassing mercy of God for loving acceptance. For the most part, our struggles, and most especially our failures, provide our pathways to kinder, more compassionate perceptions and broader, more tolerant points of view. The more deeply we probe the depths of our humanity—our own capacity for evil as well as for good—the more patient and tolerant we may become of others' weaknesses. Our capacity for compassion and understanding deepens in tandem with our sense of identity with the weakness of others.

If we know from within how it feels to be addicted to alcohol, we may well feel a special compassion toward someone who is caught in that compulsion. We may then feel drawn to help in a substance-abuse program. A woman who has experienced abuse from her spouse and has been helped to free herself from the situation feels herself motivated to take the leadership in establishing a safe house for other women in her neighborhood. A man whose daughter was brutally murdered becomes a prison chaplain noted for his compassion and his powerful protest against the death penalty.[28] Our wounds can be the source of our own transformation.

Suffering, whether from our own flaws and failures or from wounds inflicted by others, can be, paradoxically, a deep source of compassion for us. It can enhance our sensitivity to others. Suffering of any kind challenges our perennial delusion that we are in control of life. It ex-poses us—that is, it takes us out of our ordinary place or frame of mind, and forces us to see ourselves in a different light. Far from being in control, we have to acknowledge our vulnerability. Suffering, probably more than any other human experience, gives us opportunity to confront a truth about our human existence that we most often seek to avoid or deny, and that is its gift. Somehow, acknowledging our vulnerability clears our heart's channel of false pride and superiority that separate us from others. With those self-centered blocks out of the way, mercy can flow more strongly and deeply through us into the world. Vulnerability opens the path to communion.

And so our sense of solidarity with wounded humanity— indeed, with wounded and endangered members of all species—deepens as we encounter, at ever-new levels, the unavoidable phenomenon of suffering. The suffering of others, both human and that of other species, finds resonance in our own, and elicits in us a response of *com*-passion, suffering-*with*. Provided that our hearts are open, that mysterious resonance draws us toward each other in a unique kind of loving understanding and mutuality. Here we meet and experience the God of compassion, the God whose name we know, in Jesus, to be mercy. That is how our sense of communion deepens.

As Desmond Tutu wrote:

> Nelson Mandela emerged from prison not spewing words of
> hatred and revenge. He amazed us all by his heroic embodi-
> ment of reconciliation and forgiveness. . . . Those twenty-
> seven years and all the suffering they entailed were the fires of
> the furnace that tempered his steel, that removed the dross.
> Perhaps without that suffering he would have been less able
> to be as compassionate and as magnanimous as he turned out
> to be. And that suffering on behalf of others gave him an
> authority and credibility that can be provided by nothing else
> in quite the same way.[29]

Growing out of the deepening sense of communion, almost
as a twin sister, a natural tendency toward nonviolence
emerges. Paul's assertion that "if one member suffers, all suffer together with it; if one member is honored, all rejoice
together with it" (1 Cor. 12:26) becomes simple fact, a truth
we know not just in our heads, but in our own heart's experience. "In actual practice the expansion of my non-violence has
kept exact pace with that of my identification with starved
humanity," wrote Gandhi.[30]

To carry deep in our hearts this suffering condition of
humankind, and to know that we all belong to each other,
leads us to want to relieve the burdens of hatred, distrust, and
oppression that we see all around us. "I've seen too much hate
to want to hate, myself," Martin Luther King Jr. said in his
Christmas sermon on peace. "Every time I see it, I say to
myself, hate is too great a burden to bear." He continued:

> Somehow we must be able to stand up before our most bitter
> opponents and say: "We shall match your capacity to inflict
> suffering by our capacity to endure suffering. We will meet
> your physical force with soul force. Do to us what you will and
> we will still love you. . . . But be assured that we'll wear you
> down by our capacity to suffer, and one day we will win our
> freedom. We will not only win freedom for ourselves; we will

so appeal to your heart and conscience that we will win you in
the process, and our victory will be a double victory."[31]

These words of King are the fruit and the testament of a
deep life of faith in the gospel of Jesus. If humankind is to survive on planet Earth, we must very quickly develop the capacity to embrace the whole of the planet, including all of its varied
life-forms. Our hearts must be ready to endure suffering with
compassion and with nonviolent responses to aggression. That
is a special challenge for us in our U.S. culture, where greed
and violence threaten to hold us captive. We cannot change
overnight. We move little by little, as we are led.

Our faith in Jesus' revelation of God's enduring presence
in human life, especially through his death and resurrection,
tells us that we may trust that our suffering, if we bear it lovingly, yields compassion, which is the most powerful instrument of the world's healing. When we are willing to engage
life along with its suffering, we find that our own capacity for
compassion will deepen in equal measure. We are, then, living in the pattern that Jesus set. That faith is perhaps the
deepest, most important, and most precious heritage of the
Christian tradition.

If a level of trust and comfort has been cultivated in a
group over a period of time, the inner vulnerabilities, the tendencies we experience in ourselves, can be very fruitfully
shared. We learn from each other's struggles something of
the intricacy of our own ego investments, and we learn ways
to detect them. Honest identifying of our own inner landscape is the first step, and in some ways the most difficult
because of its subtlety. Willingness to expose our mistakes,
our failures, and our difficulties—or to allow them to be
exposed—is another step. Every experience of ex-posing

leaves us vulnerable, and vulnerability allows the breaking down of a barrier so that something new can enter into the newly created space. It is one small moment of "dying" that opens to new life.

An intuition, as old as the ancient Hindu Upanishads, recognizes that everything in the world about us is either food or the eater of food. Author Annie Dillard observed that every single thing she saw—daddy longlegs, grasshoppers, butterflies, birds, leaves—was at least partly nibbled:

> Is this what it's like, I thought then, and think now: a little blood here, a chomp there, and still we live, trampling the grass? Must everything whole be nibbled? Here was a new light on the intricate texture of things in the world, the actual plot of the present moment in time after the fall: the way we the living are nibbled and nibbling—not held aloft on a cloud in the air but bumbling pitted and scarred and broken through a frayed and beautiful land.[32]

Everything whole will inevitably be nibbled. And we are, always, nibbling in some fashion or other; we always live at the expense of life. Flawed as we are, our hope cannot be to separate ourselves from this process. Our hope can only be the modest intent to inflict as little damage as possible, while at the same time enhancing life by our willingness to share our own life energies for the good of others. As we have said before, that is our human way of aligning ourselves with the ongoing breaking down and building up of the universe.

But we have to be willing to see things as they are: to see the pain, the cruelty, the injustice, the brokenness. Little by little, our lens widens so that we realize our own participation, our solidarity with every part of creation that is suffering, oppressed, victimized. A sense of communion moves us, as it moved Jesus, to act with love and integrity, at whatever cost, to do whatever the situation requires of us: to resist, to advocate, to heal. It was, after all, bread *broken* that Jesus shared with his disciples, saying, "Take and eat: this is my body." Our life depends upon our capacity to ingest, to partake in that very brokenness. Our willingness to enter into that process is reengaged every time we accept the bread and wine, body and blood of Christ, in Eucharist. We agree to be the Body of Christ here and now.

Chapter Seven

Being Where We Belong

Speaking the truth in love, we must grow up in every way into Christ.

Eph. 4:15

W e turn, then, to another role that the community can play: discernment at a different level, the discernment of gifts. When he wrote to the Christian communities he had worked to form, Paul insisted that they recognize and respect the "variety of gifts of the Holy Spirit." His extended analogy of how the members of the human body work together is a perennial source of challenge and inspiration for everyone who engages in processes of community formation, community building, and community life.

Paul reminds his communities that the ear doesn't claim that it can function instead of the eye, nor does it exclude itself from participation in the functioning of the whole simply because it can't be the eye. Nor is a weaker or "less respectable" member considered of less value because its function is not so prominent. Each part has its own respected and valued role, and dissension is thus avoided.

The members all share the same care for one another's well-being. "If one member suffers, all suffer together with it; if one member is honored, all rejoice together with it." There are many gifts, many services, many activities, but "to each is given the manifestation of the Spirit for the common good" (1 Cor. 12; see also Rom. 12:3–8). It is a beautiful and helpful analogy, and it is marvelous food for meditation.

But when we do meditate on what it means to be the Body of Christ, and when we try to live it, we find that it is really quite difficult to put into practice. We encounter two distinct but related temptations, coveting and competition, which can entrap the most sincere of disciples. These temptations may seem much less heroic than were Jesus' temptations, and perhaps they are in fact only garden-variety weeds. But like the fast-growing kudzu, if not tended to, temptations can quickly take over a garden. Coveting and competing are both rooted in the impulse to enhance one's own power. They can corrupt the Body of Christ.

The book of Numbers tells of Korah, a Levite who ministered to the people who came to the sanctuary to worship. But Korah wanted to be able to enter the sanctuary as Moses and Aaron did. Korah challenged Moses and Aaron, and Moses called upon God to decide between them. In the judgment, the earth opened up and swallowed Korah and all of his family (Num. 16:1–35).

A Hasidic tale comments upon that incident in the following way:

> A disciple asked the rabbi of Kotzk what it was that caused Korah to rebel against Moses and Aaron. "He had observed," answered the rabbi, that whenever he stood up above, among the singing Levites, great gifts of the spirit descended upon him. And so he thought that if he stood within the tabernacle with his censer, still greater gifts would accrue to him. He did not know that the power he had felt came upon him because Aaron stood in his place and he in his."[33]

What a common, age-old trap! Consider this scenario, drawing on and updating the Hasidic tale. Suppose you are a member of a very active peace and justice committee in your parish. You have long had an interest in Latin America, and your parish is planning to send a team to explore the possibility of finding a "sister parish" in Guatemala. The trip, it seems, may well involve some danger, risks, and uncertainties. You long to be part of the team. Your family circumstances, however, are such that it is impossible for either you or your spouse to be gone for a three-week period. You have talked at length with the committee, but the doors seem closed. Together, you have sadly concluded that the time is simply not right.

So you try to pitch in with the preparations and planning, and sometimes you feel genuinely valuable to the group because of your practical and generous suggestions. But you find yourself often feeling resentful on a lot of levels. You resent the amount of attention and concern the team members are receiving. You resent that your spouse hasn't seemed more willing to sacrifice to make it possible for you to go. Sometimes you even resent your children, whose needs at this point are a major factor keeping you home. You feel sidelined, trapped, unimportant, useless. Sometimes you feel sorry for yourself, sometimes you imagine how much more effective a representative you would be than someone else who has been chosen for the trip. And sometimes all these feelings are compounded by a voice that says, "You shouldn't feel such things. See what a petty, sinful person you are!" Then you feel guilty on top of it all.

These imaginings come and go. You don't like them, but there they are. They can take a variety of forms, and they can play themselves out in a variety of scenarios. Sometimes they might represent you as "poor me," suffering a lack of recognition or attention. They may present you as inferior to others,

or as an incompetent, bungling fool, hopelessly stupid, para-
lyzing you with a fear of failure. On the other hand, they may
inflate your virtues, giving you a sense of heroism, grandios-
ity, excellence, or superiority, leading you to arrogance and
brashness. It doesn't matter which form they take. They are,
for the moment, keeping you focused on yourself.

What's going on here? Our egos play an essential and perfectly healthy role in shaping our energies to interact with the
outer world. But they also have some very clever ruses — often
seemingly innocent self-protective mechanisms, to get us to
focus on ourselves. They can assume multiple guises, multiple
voices.

Those voices and images are common to our experience.
They thrive upon making comparisons; they glorify or
demean: better than, more important than, less talented than,
not as smart as. . . . They lure us to covet someone else or their
gifts. They make us discontent with our own contribution.
They mislead us. They do not represent our true identity. Who
we are is something far deeper and more mysterious than any
image we have of ourselves.

So we are like Korah, not recognizing that it is our fidelity
to our own very particular role, no matter what it is, that
enables and enriches the life of the whole body. Checking our
motivation is always in order. Is it really the welfare of the
Guatemalan people that matters, or only our own spoke of
earlier? Dwelling on the sinfulness or even the possible truth
of such voices simply encourages them to sink their roots
deeper. The only useful response is to try to name it, become
aware of the voice as a voice, or the feeling as a feeling — and
then to ignore it, not to feed it with attention, change the subject. Focusing on an outer reality or paying attention to something immediate that needs to be done can bring attention

back to the reality of the present moment in a wholesome way. And always, in a quick inner motion, simply remember the Mercy that lies at the ground of all that is, and breathe it in.

As we have said, attending to our thoughts and feelings is steady, hard work, requiring discipline. But it is work that we all do over and over again, in new and different contexts, all our lives. It is work that we want to learn to do skillfully, clearing the channel so that, as each of us is quietly and faithfully doing just what we are given to do, the dance troupe of which we are a part is performing smoothly, contributing to the beauty and harmony of the whole. If we try to do somebody else's step, we cause a disruption of the ensemble. We each have to learn the dance movements that make up our own particular part of the dance, and learn to synchronize our movements in graceful participation.

The second trap, competition, is very similar, though it presents itself in slightly different guise. Competitive feelings apparently arose even among Jesus' disciples, in his presence! At one point, according to Luke, "an argument arose among them as to which one of them was the greatest." Jesus answered by setting a child in their midst (Lk. 9:46). Mark records that on another occasion, James and John pulled Jesus aside to ask a favor of him. They wanted to find out if they couldn't get Jesus to promise them special seats next to him in "his glory." (In Matthew's Gospel, their mother makes the request.) The other disciples resented this attempt at self-promotion. Jesus had to try, over and over again, to get them to understand that assigning "first places" was no part of his mission. Rather, he said, "Whoever wishes to become great among you must be your servant, and whoever wishes to be first among you must be slave of all . . ." (Mk. 10:35–45; Mt. 20:20).

Anyone intent upon following the way of Jesus is familiar with these words. Anyone intent upon following the way of Jesus is also familiar with how difficult they can be to put into practice. Especially in this culture, competition is a way of life.

To prove oneself, to win, to be somebody, to succeed in some demonstrable and recognizable way, especially financially—we imbibe these cultural values from childhood on. Not to be lured by them is nearly impossible. We need to be very discerning and relentlessly honest about our own motives, and we need each other to help us do that.

Competition is basically about power, about superiority. But Jesus and his followers are motivated by a different S/spirit. Clearly, Jesus' teaching is about making one's unique contribution, whatever it may be; it's not about being in charge. It's about helping others to succeed, not about getting glory for oneself. It's about cooperating so that we all win, not about competing so that I/we win and others lose. It's about freeing and empowering others rather than acquiring power for oneself. How can community members enable each other to stay on track?

Fundamentally, the group works to develop a sensitivity to noticing and encouraging each other's gifts. Obviously, this takes time, patience, attentiveness, mutual acceptance, and a generous spirit. It is really a question of educing, of drawing out those particular capacities that lie within each one, and of genuinely valuing them. For each individual, deep inner attentiveness is required, listening carefully to one another to learn where their gifts or leanings may lie. Often enough, we can name for another a gift that they themselves would not have recognized, which may simply need to be brought into the light of awareness. Our sensitivity involves listening for cues from the group that resonate with our own leanings, and also the internal process of monitoring. This is no simple matter. We have noted that when we listen inwardly, we likely hear many voices telling us what we should be and do, how we ought to look or feel or act, what we need to have, what we need to do to be somebody. But besides those internal voices, there are so many needs, so many calls from the world around us, so many committees to join, so many good causes to contribute to, and they all communicate a sense of urgency. The risk is double-edged: We can become so involved running from meeting to meeting that we begin to neglect our primary responsibilities to our families. We can stretch ourselves so thin that we are fragmented and impatient and resentful. Or we can feel guilty that we are so limited and blame ourselves for selfishness or laziness and for not doing more.

Somewhere in the midst of that noisy throng of voices, when we quiet ourselves to pray or to journal or to listen, either alone or in company with friends, the voice of the Spirit will be heard: nudging, encouraging, challenging. Contrary to the voices that come from media glitz, this voice often connects us with suffering, with a need. It's a need that takes root in one's heart and often returns to mind, especially in times of quiet. Is it something I can do, congruent with my responsibilities? Is it something I am drawn to do? Fear, resistance, and anxiety are not necessarily reasons to reject the invitation. Those feelings may simply be putting me in touch with the blocks that try to protect me from risk of failure. A trusted group of friends can help to clarify the confusion.

Discernment is never a matter of "figuring it out" rationally, or of letting the schedule or the checkbook decide. Rather, discernment is a process of allowing a kind of gestalt to emerge, one that seems to involve the whole person—feelings, heart, mind, spirit. If we have prayed for openness, and the concern continues to lie on our heart, then it may be time to move to connect the concern with the need. Frequently, it will feel like something we *must* do: not to respond would seem to betray our deepest sense of self before God. We cannot *not* do it. This we understand as a "call."

Calling, however, can happen in many different ways. Sometimes it seems to be action that takes the lead; other times it may be thinking. A retired person, for instance, somewhat casually decides—really because she has nothing else to do—to go along when her friend visits in a prison outside town. She meets a prisoner whose condition appalls her, and whose story touches her heart. She goes a second time, and a third, and each time her sense of responsibility and commitment deepens. That initial experience leads her to advocacy on this prisoner's behalf; she begins to confront the criminal justice system.

Maybe someone reads or hears about the militarizing of outer space. He finds himself thinking often about its implications for the future of his children; when he prays, the issue lies on his heart. He starts by writing to his congresspersons, and finally joins a group that works to expose the dangers and illegitimacy of such activities in outer space . . . and little by little he is confronting the military-industrial complex. Thinking and acting operate in reciprocal fashion. No matter which seems to come first, one can lead to the other.

Sometimes we carry a concern in our hearts for a long time, but simply do not know what to do about it. Dorothy Day was already keenly aware of her own sensitivity to social justice issues when she went as a reporter to Washington DC in 1932 to cover the hunger march. Once a Communist, she had become a Catholic. Watching the crowd of men and women at the demonstration, she was overtaken with a deeply disturbing sense of the inadequacy of reporting on this Communist-inspired protest against poverty. Where was the church? Her heart was filled with a painful longing to do something more. It was the Feast of the Immaculate Conception, and she went to the National Shrine and prayed, "with tears and with anguish that some way would open up for me to use the talents I possessed for my fellow workers, for the poor." With the kind of timing that is the hallmark of God's providence, she returned to New York the next day to discover Peter Maurin waiting for her. Maurin would be the catalyst for their beginning what would become the Catholic Worker Movement, still one of the most radical witnesses to a lifestyle of voluntary poverty, pacifism, and advocacy for social justice in U.S. history. It was, apparently, the intensity of Dorothy Day's willing commitment and her prayer that opened the door.[34]

How we get involved is not important. What matters is that we are listening, inwardly and outwardly, with hearts open to respond.

If, in our deepest intent, we seek to be faithful to God's call to follow Jesus, we need not be afraid of making mistakes. We may sometimes have to go through the pain or discomfort of having taken what seems to be a wrong turn, but we can trust that that misstep will be integrated into the pattern. Remember: we are ourselves in process, and part of a larger process that involves breaking down and re-creating, dying and rising. When we make a mistake, we learn something about who we are not. And much, perhaps most of our learning in this deep area of our identity is learning by elimination.

It is often by experiencing the falsity and discomfort of what is not true for us, of trying unsuccessfully and unhappily to be what we are not, or to do what is not given to us, that we clear the pathway to who we really are. Our deepest identity is quite simple, but in fact we never access it directly. It is the place within us where God dwells in mystery, the place where Love lives in us and yearns to find expression in the world. It is the place of compassion, compassion that opens us to communion. We discover it only in the painful process of learning to love: we die a little at a time, and each dying opens us to deeper love. It takes a lifetime.

If we are faithful and attentive, our potential is drawn into connection with a place of need within the whole body. The fact that it is ours to do does not mean that it will always be smooth or easy. Even with discernment, all resistance may not be set to rest; one may still feel anxiety or fear of inadequacy. There may be conflict ahead; the call may be to prophetic confrontation that leaves us wounded and scarred. There may be a price to pay, calling for a courage we do not know we have. It is, after all, the way of Jesus.

Often, though, even in the midst of trouble, we may be aware of a sense of integrity, of being faithful to a very deep truth of our own being. Out of that sense of grounding in truth will come the strength, the conviction, the courage to stand our ground, to face what comes, to speak the truth, to love in spite of everything. And not to give up.

The truth is that no matter how showy or how behind-the-scenes, how important or how insignificant our gift may seem, it is integral to the whole.

As Paul taught, gifts differ. Each of us has a gift that is completely unique but which, if we are faithful, makes its particular, necessary contribution to the whole.

A story from the early desert fathers tells of a visitor to Egypt who wished to see two famous teachers, Abba Arsenius and Abba Moses. The visitor found Arsenius in his home, but the holy man paid no attention to him. So after a while, he went to visit Moses, who greeted him gladly, visited with him, and sent him off with a happy heart. Someone, hearing of this, was puzzled and prayed:

> "Lord, explain this matter to me: for Thy name's sake the one flees from [human beings] and the other, for Thy name's sake, receives them with open arms." Then two large boats were shown to him on a river and he saw Abba Arsenius and the Spirit of God sailing in one, in perfect peace; and in the other was Abba Moses with the angels of God, and they were all eating honey cakes.[35]

To be comfortable with and grateful for one's own gift, whatever it is, requires humility—living in the awareness that our life is, at every moment, a gift; that it does not belong to us; that it is given to us so that we can share it with the whole. To have the sense of "being where one belongs, doing what one is given to do" is one of the most liberating experiences of life, and one of life's greatest blessings, whether it involves peace or honey cakes.

That blessing is always available to us, even in the hard times, if we can learn to live trusting in the merciful love that is holding the whole creation in being, always intent on bringing life out of death. When we stop trusting, we become uneasy: we shift to relying on our own resources, thinking that somehow we have to get it right and that we have to save ourselves. It is not so. We do have to set ourselves to be faithful to our baptismal and eucharistic commitments, to be willing to participate as lovingly as we can in that life-giving process of dying to self. That is all. God does the rest.

The Challenge of Global Justice

In my flesh I am completing what is lacking in Christ's
afflictions for the sake of his body, that is, the church.

Col. 1:24

The human species is a magnificent creation. We have been
able to transcend almost all boundaries or limitations on
our mobility, even to the extent of leaving the planet to walk
on the moon. Soon, according to present plans, we will have
military installations on Mars. We are able to experiment with
all kinds of technological gadgets, artificial intelligence, means
of communication, and genetic modifications, even though
we have no possible way of foreseeing the consequences. We
can replace damaged hearts (at least the physical ones) and
rebuild limbs.

But we are also the only species that hasn't learned to live
in its niche. Because we are so mobile, we can destroy incal-
culable numbers of other species without even thinking
about it. In fact, we can destroy the whole planet in no time
flat. We have a sense that there is no limit to what we can do.
What on earth *is* the appropriate role of the human species?

I suggested earlier that our Creator God has given
humans the potential to transform the whole of creation into
a harmonious unity, a communion of life grounded in an all-
encompassing Divine Love. Because we are capable of
increasingly expansive loving awareness, broad enough to
include in some detail the composition of the whole planet,
our role is to serve the magnificent Mystery of Life, in its

various manifestations, on planet Earth. It appears, then, that the kind of caring that is implied in the words "justice" or "right relations" must extend to the whole world.

What might we learn from less industrialized cultures, which rely on personal attitudes of forgiveness and receptiveness to set the context for the practice of justice? In such cultures, people realize that they must continue to live together. Now, with the broad frame of planetary citizenship, we know that the very survival of life on planet Earth depends upon our ability to recognize our human kinship with all the other species. How do we cultivate this new awareness?

Such an attitude would presume a sense of responsibility to protect and enhance the reciprocal processes that maintain life on Earth. It would require attention to mending and restoring those processes when suffering reveals that they have been violated. Because the whole globe is threatened, we have to build global coalitions to work together for peace and justice and ecological sensitivity. Our tasks include work to develop an interspecies ethic of compassion for the whole community of life, and a system of law that encompasses the whole. All of this is now clearly the agenda for right relations, for justice.

But we cannot love "all species" in the abstract. "Care" is a word that has to be concretized. So where do we begin?

We begin where we are, starting right here with our own minds and hearts and spirits. It begins with minds and hearts that are open to appreciate the reality of the other without prejudice, open to seeing truth from many points of view, wherever and in whatever form it may appear. It begins with readiness to recognize our common spiritual and humane values, our human aspirations and our hopes, and to welcome whatever will truly lead to our unifying. Our work begins with minds and hearts and spirits open to love.

So, what does it mean to be the Body of Christ in a global society? What does it mean to be a Christian committed to working for justice on planet Earth? How will we see, how will we know what we need to do?

As Quaker John Woolman (1720–1772) wrote, "Love [is] the first motion."[36] We listen for cries of pain which echo in our hearts, see who is suffering, see where violence and inequity are disrupting relationships, as does the God of Israel, as does the God of Jesus Christ. The injustice, the need, the systems' failures: these are the privileged loci for hearing the voice of God that will open our hearts.

There is no real substitute for hands-on experience to broaden the capacity to love. We may be able to trace in our own lives an experience of witnessing a flagrant violation of justice, or simply encountering someone in need, which, perhaps in surprising or difficult ways, expanded the boundaries of our heart. Somehow, in that experience, we were inwardly moved from simply looking, we were ex-posed, moved to a new position, out of our usual, familiar position as spectator. Suddenly we were seeing with the heart and finding a resonance within ourselves. We felt a sense of caring, of kinship, of oneness in the plight of that person. Something was given, something drew us. We felt "called." That is how we enter the path to communion.

"Love is the first motion." In his journal, John Woolman recorded the movement of his spirit as he responded to its nudging to spend time sojourning among the Indians who dwelt in the New England area. He engaged in lengthy soul searching, alone and with his wife. Always somewhat somber, he experienced many moments of self-doubt. He feared risking the real dangers involved. There were times of intense physical as well as mental suffering. He consulted with

Friends' meetings and, "having the unity of Friends," he continued to move forward. He chanced to find a friend who felt a like drawing, and step by step they undertook the difficult journey. Reflecting on his own "process," Woolman wrote,

> Love was the first motion, and thence a concern arose to spend some time with the Indians, that I might feel and understand their life and the spirit they live in, if haply I might receive some instruction from them, or they might be in any degree helped forward by my following the leadings of truth among them. . . .[37]

Notice the motivation: first, love. Woolman's intent springs from a sense of mutuality, of reciprocity: there would be something he could learn from them, and perhaps something of his own attempt to live his truth in their midst might be helpful to them. No attitude of do-gooder pity or superiority here, but rather a willingness to share, to learn. It is an attitude of openness, a capacity to appreciate the other.

Woolman's whole life was characterized by that kind of sensitivity and attentiveness to the needs around him, and a continual posture of listening and watching inwardly for an indication that God was nudging him to do something about them. The needs in the outer world were met by an attitude of willingness and deep inner reflection.

Much of Woolman's life was shaped by his concern about the system of slavery, practiced at the time by Friends in the area. Woolman saw clearly the evil and injustice of the system, and he could not keep silent. He went from person to person, house to house, quietly raising questions, voicing that concern. Slowly, person by person, the group's consciousness shifted. Eventually, Friends' meetings became vocal advocates of abolition. One person's courage and fidelity to truth made the difference.

Later, Woolman's concerns included not only the enslavement of humans, but also the suffering of animals, like the fowl cooped up on the ship during his voyage to England, or the horses who were harshly used in the English stagecoaches. He spoke of concern about the wasteful use of timber and the killing of whales. He wrote,

> I believe where the love of God is verily perfected, and the true spirit of government watchfully attended to, a tenderness towards all creatures made subject to us will be experienced, and a care felt in us that we do not lessen that sweetness of life in the animal creation which the great Creator intends for them under our government.[38]

"Not to lessen that sweetness of life in the animal creation which the great Creator intends for them . . ."—spoken like a twenty-first-century ecologist! Love is the first motion, and then begins a life devoted to justice: doing whatever one is drawn to do to ease the plight of living beings who suffer, to repair the violations of their integrity, to reconcile and alleviate the inequalities. In such actions, in putting himself there, his own heart opened more and more deeply in compassion, and he lived more and more deeply in union with God and the whole creation. Reflecting on his sojourn among the Indians, Woolman wrote, "A near sympathy with them was raised in me, and, my heart being enlarged in the love of Christ, I thought that the affectionate care of a good man for his only brother in affliction does not exceed what I then felt for that people." Woolman's heart had responded to "a kinship appeal."[39]

John Woolman is amazingly instructive for us at this time in our history. His life illustrates many of the components that characterize the life of a member of the Body of Christ who is committed to acting for justice: the congruence between inner willingness to place one's life in service (love), and outer attentiveness to the world; consistent attention to truth, both his own inner truth and the truth that prodded him, in his scriptural meditations and his prayer, to act; consulting with family and friends, and making sure that he is acting in concord with the larger community of the church. His life embodied a sensitivity to any violation of right relationships. His empathetic heart saw what others did not see, and led him to actions both of creative nonviolent resistance, breaking down barriers, and of opening new sensitivities in the human conscience. Paul had described the body of Christ: "If one member suffers, all suffer together with it; if one member is honored, all rejoice together with it" (1 Cor. 12:26). John Woolman experienced that reality. His life was a journey of compassion into communion.

But John Woolman lived in a different, far less complex time. In this century of worldwide communications systems and worldwide capacities for destruction, what are the signs of the times that we need to read? What characterizes our action for justice?

Action for justice must take on a global character, and must happen on many levels. Following the universal pattern of breakdown and re-creation, actions will take the form of both resistance and innovation, each imbued with the creative, nonviolent energy of the Spirit's impetus toward deeper unity.

There are many avenues of resistance. It is possible now that global communications can facilitate simultaneous protest demonstrations all around the world, as happened in 2003 and 2004 in resistance to the U.S. occupation of Iraq. We have seen people from all around the globe gather to protest, with some success, the policies of the World Trade Organization and the International Monetary Fund. Those protests seemed to empower some smaller countries to unite to withstand the pressure of the global giants. When moral suasion does not succeed, it is possible to concentrate on specific international corporations whose record of environmental destruction or manufacturing policies are well known, and to design boycotts and protests that expose those policies in such a way as to make their continuance economically infeasible. The stranglehold of greed and militarism that dominates the world is now the Egypt in our scenario of global exodus journey to liberation and justice. Even when such methods of resistance seem ineffective in changing systems, they build a sense of solidarity that will, inevitably, create conditions for change. Even giants can be incapacitated by a sufficient quantity of gnats.

On the positive front, global coalitions are being built that promote coexistence and cooperation. People from all over the world participate in the World Social Forum, which engages creative thinkers from different races, nationalities, and languages, to imagine together how the world *might* be, and what steps we can take to get from here to there. Projects in microlending in poor countries, cottage industries, international networks to market fair-trade products: these and countless others testify to the growing number of persons aware of global injustices, and willing to invest time and energy to invent channels of communication so that, step by step, some of these inequities can be restored by right relations.

If we are to be effective, the Body of Christ must recognize its global connections. The "catholicity" of the Roman Catholic Church has never been more important, for we have links everywhere on the globe that can provide information and opportunity. U.S. parishes link with parishes in Central America or Eastern Europe, and genuine mutual learning and exchange occurs.

But still more, our Catholic networks will join hands with other Christian communions, and we will all join hands with persons of other traditions whose approaches may be very different from our own, but who see the critical need for us to recognize our common humanity. We have to deconstruct the barriers that we have allowed to separate us. It is a broad kind of new "ecumenism," which will demand disciplines of tolerance, humility, and willingness to learn from open dialogue, not just in matters of faith but in the whole gamut of political and cultural assumptions.[40] And dialogue means not just convincing the other of my truth, but being willing to risk changes in my own positions that may threaten my sense of security.

Besides the global scene, there are urgent calls for resistance nationally and locally. Power—the power of violence— has grown among us to a national obsession. The issues are familiar to us: resistance to war and the militarization of space, continuing investments in nuclear bombs and weapons of mass destruction, trade policies that make it impossible for workers to earn a living wage, and labor policies that violate the rights of labor to organize. Continuing racism, gender discrimination, and homophobia keep whole populations in positions of powerlessness, inferiority, and often fear. It is probably safe to say that every single system in this country's infrastructure is riddled with problems and dysfunctions that cause pain not only to the human species but other members of the community of life as well. There is a massive amount of injustice in this country that needs to be addressed, and the Holy Spirit is surely at work prompting group and individual efforts to raise consciousness and to provide a dissenting voice.

On the positive side, there is increasing evidence that a new population is emerging with a unifying vision of a different world. Many initiatives are being undertaken to create alternatives: alternative energy projects, alternative industry, alternative building construction, medicine, agriculture, education, transportation—alternative everything! There has for a long time been talk of a Department of Peace to balance the nation's Department of Defense and the power of the Pentagon. In many places, local people organize co-ops as markets for food or other goods that can be handled locally and can manage to break loose, at least to some extent, from dependence on large corporate chains. Not every project will succeed. What matters is that humans begin to enact a new vision, and to channel our creativity into positive ventures that may hold hope for a better future for us all.

And on the level closest to home, there are our own lifestyles that are inevitably enmeshed with the systemic injustice that permeates our culture. Everything we have spoken of in the preceding pages relates to our lifestyles, shaped by our priorities, our commitments. What habits do we cultivate that are consciously countercultural? How trapped have we become in the frenetic pace; how controlled are we by the status quo? How careful are we to try to identify our own tendency to greed, to have more than we need; what ways have we found to discern the difference between need and want? How do we allow the obsession with consuming to infiltrate our families? How closely do we monitor our own use of TV and computers and that of our children? How careful are we about violence in our attitudes, words, and behaviors; what conscious efforts do we make to learn skills of nonviolence? How committed are we to trying to build community in our own surroundings? How much time do we spend together as families, so that the children really have a chance to appreciate the value of some alternative ways of approaching life, alternative attitudes toward being and having? How seriously do we regard the need for quiet and reflection, for genuine friendship and sharing? In sum, how seriously do we take the gospel of Jesus?

Daniel Maguire suggests that the biblical vision is "prescriptive of a new humanity with new social arrangements geared to the elimination of poverty, to ending all oppression, and to the flourishing of life on this versatile earth." He continues:

> This liberative viewpoint rings with contemporaneity. Jesus' teaching on loving enemies has for a long time and often seemed hopelessly idealistic. Given today's military potential it may contain the seeds of our last, best, and most practical hope. [It may contain] the moral and political mutation required now for the survival of the species.[41]

"Our last, best hope for the survival of the species." Those are strong, serious words. If there is even a shred of truth in Maguire's assertion, will we, the members of the Body of Christ, rise to the challenge of giving that hope a chance to bud, to blossom, to flourish in our imperiled world?

It is a staggering task. The need for supportive connections is greater than ever. We need others to help keep alive these alternative values and commitments within us and for us. We do not take on the task by ourselves; there are innumerable pockets of hope and resistance all around the world. We need them to carry the hope when we are discouraged, and to be assured that we aren't crazy when we feel alone in our efforts to live from a different set of values. We need them to keep our imaginations reaching for alternatives, stretching toward the possible.

We need the witness and company of others to give us the resilience and courage to stay steady. And finally, we need to be empowered: we need to know that even our small steps, individually or as a group, really do make a difference. We need to be confident beyond doubt that we are each one a small, *very* small but irreplaceable unit in a beautiful, divinely choreographed Dance of Love.

The good news of Jesus is that there is available to us a source of security that is infinitely more reliable than anything the society can imagine: a God who has promised to be with us, and who will not give up on us. We know a God who has pledged to us that if we will risk the venture—perhaps into the desert or to the cross—we will have the courage, the support, and the wisdom that we need. Our faith is in God who is actually working within and among us, encouraging and sustaining us in times of suffering, drawing us forward into a future that we have not yet imagined. And we will not be overwhelmed by the task.

In the words of Thomas Kelly,

> [God] in our truest moments . . . disquiets us with the world's needs. By inner persuasions He draws us to a few very definite tasks, our tasks, God's burdened heart particularizing His burdens in us.[42]

And Kelly speaks of

> the special responsibility experienced in a concern. For a Quaker concern particularizes this cosmic tenderness. It

brings to a definite and effective focus in some concrete task all that experience of love and responsibility which might evaporate, in its broad generality, into yearnings for a golden Paradise.[43]

This "concern," then, is not a generalized sentiment, not simply emotion. It is the particular, the do-able, which is felt as one's own calling, given by God. It is tailored to our own condition and situation:

The loving Presence does not burden us equally with all things, but considerately puts upon each of us just a few central tasks, as emphatic responsibilities.

Kelly says that we may experience a

universal concern for all the multitude of good things that need doing. Toward them all we feel kindly, but we are dismissed from active service in most of them. And we have an easy mind in the presence of desperately real needs which are not our direct responsibility. We cannot die on every cross, nor are we expected to.[44]

"We cannot die on every cross, nor are we expected to." We have within us the continual presence of the Holy Spirit, the Spirit of Jesus, who Jesus promised would "guide you into all the truth" (Jn. 14:16–17; 16:13, 26). That Spirit works in each of us, nudging us to recognize our gift and put it at the service of life. We can rely on that presence most especially when we gather in Jesus' name: "Where two or three are gathered in my name, I am there among them" (Mt. 18:20). We can count on that presence through the church, through the whole Body of Christ, for Jesus promised, "I am with you always, to the end of the age" (Mt. 28:20). And we are learning to develop sensitivity to that same Holy Spirit, permeating the universe, appearing in diverse forms in diverse cultures, always creating longing within us to know, finally, the communion of oneness.

Paul saw the whole of creation, and us humans as well, "groaning in labor pains." He envisioned a hope that "the creation itself will be set free from its bondage to decay and will obtain the freedom of the glory of the children of God" (Rom. 8:19–23). Perhaps now, in a new way, with the three lenses of science, of justice/solidarity, and of communion, we can glimpse what that freedom might involve. It asks us to commit ourselves to participate in that process of redemption, each in our own way, and all together, spending our lives in the service of life. The whole of creation, with painful setbacks and sudden surges, longs with the longing of God to be drawn forward toward transformation into a communion of love. Can that vision inspire us, can it sustain our hope? That is our faith. It calls us to keep in our hearts a continual prayer to *know* the unity. And it calls us to *act*.

Afterword

The Dance Goes On. . . .

I like to imagine the universe as
a Cosmic Dance.
It helps me keep in my mind the "big picture,"
the whole cosmos engaged
in changing
and exchanging,
always shifting.

Some patterns seem to emerge;
others are imperceptible.
But always, the discerning eye
can find a certain beauty,
a certain integrity
in the movement.
One learns to trust the process.

At each moment of history,
every single creature in the cosmos is
in the Dance.
On planet Earth, it is critical
that each dancer become familiar
with the particular dance —
appropriate to the particular troupe
and location,
the particular piece the troupe
is engaged to perform.

We have to recognize
that our individual performances will
in a flash
be swept into context of the Great Dance
whose design is far
beyond our comprehension.

But that is not to say
that each minuscule performance
is not crucial;
for each is,
at every moment, unique,
making its own irreplaceable
contribution.

Each dancer must do the best
to be in the right place
at the right time,
right on cue
on the beat;
not stumbling into position,
bumping into the other dancers
making them miss the beat;
not vying with another troupe,
trying to imitate
somebody else's step.

The very willingness
to engage with others,
to be willing to keep learning,
to practice:
somehow all of that,
not perfection,
enhances the beauty of the Dance.

Each dancer has
an irreplaceable role.
When aligned with the pattern of the Dance,
there is a place in the troupe
waiting for this particular dancer,
this particular dance step.
An empty place awaits
the entry of this particular troupe.
It doesn't matter if it's in the front row
or the back row,
or perhaps sewing costumes.
Each single participant contributes to the beauty
or the dissonance
of the whole.

No performance is ever
wasted,
The emerging shape and design is

perhaps ever-so-slightly
irrevocably affected
by the manner in which each participates.

Dancers must remember that
no one is ever alone.
No matter how isolated they feel they are,
no one has a solo performance.
No matter how singular and heroic,
how invisible and seemingly ineffective,
each dancer is irreplaceable.
No matter what the dancer does or
doesn't do,
the effect is registered,
clumsy mistakes are caught up,
integrated into the developing design
of the Whole.

The Choreographer took
risks
in the design of this Great Dance.
Simply patterned at its beginning,
the Dance increasingly involved more
and more
flexibility, requiring
improvisation,
skilled free-form dancing.

The newest dancers had to learn more
and more routines.
They had to trust
the value of their performance.
They also had to honor
their partners
and other members of the troupe,
willing to anticipate
and respond to others' every step.

The newest members,
the humans,
needed to develop keen attentiveness,
eyes and ears
and hearts open to the cues.
Their role required preparation,
so that they perform gracefully,
in sync.
It required that each be aware
of the uniqueness
of their individual role,
appreciating as well
the role of the troupe in the aesthetics
and effectiveness of the larger movement.
For these latecomers
It took time to develop skills.
Sometimes it seemed that the Dance would fold

completely;
sometimes
member troupes were trampled,
squeezed out.
But the Dance goes on:
old patterns change to yield new ones;
changing,
integrating,
changing . . .
the Dance goes on. . . .

Notes

1. Kevin W. Kelley, ed., *The Home Planet* (Reading, MA: Addison Wesley Publishing Co., 1988). For quotations in this paragraph see Sections 38, 42–45, 76, 84.
2. See http://www.earthjurisprudence.net.
3. The development of Catholic social thought summarized below can be found in Fred Kammer, S.J., *Doing Faithjustice: An Introduction to Catholic Social Thought* (Mahwah, NJ: Paulist Press, 1991), 77–120. See also Marvin L. Krier Mich, *Catholic Social Teaching and Movements* (Mystic, CT: Twenty-Third Publications, 1998).
4. While I speak here of solidarity as a human capacity, we need to appreciate the fact that other species are, in their own ways, capable of solidarity as well. Because we always risk projecting our own feelings onto other species, it is difficult for humans to speak in any adequate way of what solidarity means to other creatures. But there seems to be good evidence of maternal and paternal "care," of the value of cooperation and companionship and many other such qualities, which must be considered.
5. Quoted by Sarah Ann Sharkey, O.P., in *Earth, Our Home: Biblical Witness in the Hebrew Scriptures* (San Antonio, TX: Sor Juana Press, 2004), 39. According to Sharkey, the publication source is unknown.
6. Ibid., 33ff.
7. Although the use of inclusive language is critically important to the writer, I have tried to maintain accuracy in quoting Scripture.

    There is simply no way of avoiding the patriarchal bias of the Hebrew (and the Christian) scriptural texts, the pervasive influence of which is itself an issue of justice. We have done our best to focus on the biblical view of "right relations," but the glaring omission of reference to women in Israel's history, the omission of the feminine in its dominant ways of naming God, and the inequality of women's rights in its laws must be noted as serious and damaging limitations. "Right relations" would surely demand that the experience and influence of women be integrated in the tradition.

8. In this chapter I draw on Rabbi Sacks's interpretation of Judaism's respect for diversity; see Jonathan Sacks, *The Dignity of Difference: How to Avoid the Clash of Civilizations* (New York: Continuum, 2002). Sacks's argument, throughout the book, is that "the God of Abraham is the God of all mankind, but the faith of Abraham is not the faith of all mankind" (53). God's revelation in the Hebrew scriptures is that "God is the God of all humanity, but no single faith is or should be the faith of all humanity" (55). "We serve God, the author of diversity, by respecting diversity" (56). The Jewish tradition, he proposes, can embody the path toward genuine religious plurality.

9. God's blessing upon hospitality to strangers is embedded in Israel's nomadic past. In one account (Gen. 18:1–19) it was in the context of Abraham's hospitality to strangers that Sarah's unexpected pregnancy was foretold, fulfilling God's promise that Abraham would become "a great and mighty nation" in whom "all the nations of the earth shall be blessed." In the earlier account (Gen. 17:15–22) it was Sarah who would "give rise to the nations." In the words of Daniel Maguire, "There is no little symbolic import in the fact that the whole hope of Israel is set in a context of munificence to strangers" (*The Moral Core of Judaism and Christianity* [Minneapolis: Augsburg Fortress Press, 1993], 214).

10. Ibid., 119.

11. Many commentators believe that these passages have been added serially, at later dates, by subsequent editors. Though it was always in tension with the strain of Jewish particularism, "the Isaian tradition is one of the most powerful vectors of the broader and more inclusive way of thinking about God's saving purpose for the world," according to Joseph Blenkinsopp. See Isaiah 1–39, translation, introduction, and commentary by

Joseph Blenkinsopp, *The Anchor Bible,* vol. 19 (New York: Doubleday, 2000), 317–20.

12. For an excellent study of the historical context of the life of Mary of Nazareth, see Elizabeth A. Johnson, *Truly Our Sister: A Theology of Mary in the Communion of Saints* (New York: Continuum, 2003).

13. See Walter Wink, *The Powers That Be: Theology for a New Millennium* (New York: Doubleday, 1998), chap. 5, "Jesus' Third Way," esp. 101–11.

14. Larry L. Rasmussen, *Earth Community, Earth Ethics* (Mary-knoll, NY: Orbis Books, 1996), 252.

15. Albert Nolan, *Jesus before Christianity* (Maryknoll, NY: Orbis Books, 1976), 117 and 123.

16. See Maguire, *The Moral Core of Judaism and Christianity,* 143.

17. For a full account of the process, see Desmond M. Tutu, *No Future without Forgiveness* (New York: Doubleday Image Book, 1999).

18. For an account of the truth commission process in East Timor, see http://www.easttimor-reconciliation.org.

19. *Waterlily* (Lincoln: University of Nebraska Press, 1988), 189–94. While the narrative is fictionalized, the author is herself a Sioux and an accomplished ethnologist thoroughly familiar with the Dakota culture and its social system.

20. Adapted from "When We Are Reconciled, Then We Are Free," by Stanley W. Green in *Missions NOW* (Spring 2002), 2. The story was originally recounted by Presbyterian pastor Maake Masango.

21. See Kammer, *Faithjustice,* 99.

22. Films are sometimes a very helpful medium for making us conscious of the chain of connections, and also of the persistence, courage, and yes, humor that are required. *Erin Brokovich,* for instance, and the documentaries of Michael Moore are excellent examples.

23. See Sarah van Gelder, "Upshifters: Pioneers of an Awakening Culture," in *Yes! A Journal of Positive Futures* (1996), 38.

24. For an excellent study of the tendency of corporate power to turn demonic, see Wink, *The Powers That Be,* chap. 1, esp. 13–36.

25. Maguire, *The Moral Core of Judaism and Christianity*, 173, 174.

26. Nikos Kazantzakis, *St. Francis* (New York: Simon & Schuster, 1962), 348.

27. Thomas Merton, *The Hidden Ground of Love: The Letters of Thomas Merton on Religious Experience and Social Concerns*, ed. William H. Shannon (New York: Harcourt Brace Jovanovich, 1985), 297, 296.

28. The inspiring story of Paul Stevens is told by Judy Morris, OP, in "Murder Victim's Dad Becomes Death Row Chaplain," *St. Anthony Messenger* (July 1997), 36–41.

29. Tutu, *No Future without Forgiveness*, 39.

30. Mahatma Gandhi, *Gandhi on Non-violence*, ed. and with introduction by Thomas Merton (New York: New Directions, 1964), 48.

31. Martin Luther King Jr., *Testament of Hope: The Essential Writings of Martin Luther King, Jr.*, ed. James M. Washington (San Francisco: Harper & Row, 1986), 256–57.

32. Annie Dillard, *Pilgrim at Tinker Creek* (New York: Harper & Row, 1974), 227.

33. Martin Buber, *Tales of the Hasidim: Later Masters* (New York: Schocken Books, 1972), 274.

34. William D. Miller, *Dorothy Day: A Biography* (San Francisco: Harper & Row, 1982), 224ff.

35. Roberta Bondi, *To Love As God Loves* (Minneapolis: Fortress Press, 1987), 11–12, citing Apoth., Arsenius 38, 17–18.

36. John Woolman, *The Journal of John Woolman* (New York: Corinth Books, 1961), 142.

37. Ibid.

38. Ibid., 205.

39. Ibid., 152.

40. Though limited by the caveat that they would need to be "purged of evil associations" and "raised to a higher level" by Christian missionaries, Vatican Council II, in 1965, recognized "those elements of truth and grace which are found among peoples and which are, as it were, a sort of secret presence of God" ["Decree on the Church's Missionary Activity, para. 9, 823]. And even more strongly:

> *Throughout history even to the present day, there is found among different peoples a certain awareness of a hidden power, which lies behind the course of nature and the events of human life. At times there is even a recognition of a supreme being, or still more of a Father. This awareness and recognition results in a way of life that is imbued with a deep religious sense. . . .*
>
> *The Catholic Church rejects nothing of what is true and holy in these religions. She has a high regard for the manner of life and conduct, the precepts and doctrines which, although differing in many ways from her own teaching, nevertheless reflect a ray of that truth which enlightens all men.*

("Declaration on the Relation of the Church to Non-Christian Religions," para. 2, 739)

Vatican Council II: The Conciliar and Post-Conciliar Documents, gen. ed., Austin Flannery, OP (Wilmington, DE: Scholarly Resources Inc., 1975).

41. Maguire, *The Moral Core of Judaism and Christianity,* 83.
42. Thomas R. Kelly, *A Testament of Devotion* (New York: Harper & Brothers Publishers, 1941), 71–72, emphasis in original.
43. Ibid., 108.
44. Ibid., 109.

Index